SCOTTISH CRIME AND PUNISHMENT

INTRODUCTION

"Gentlemen, the charge against the prisoner is murder, and the punishment for murder is death, and that simple statement is sufficient to suggest to you the awful nature of the occasion which brings you and me face to face".

This was the famous opening sentence often used by defence advocates in their address to the jury when capital punishment was the ultimate penalty in our courts.

During the nineteenth century — the period largely covered by this book — more than 240 men and women kept a date with the hangman in Scotland.

The offences for which they had been found guilty ranged through murder, rape, housebreaking, fire-raising, treason, piracy, hamesucken (violence against a householder on his own property), to opening other people's letters, theft of money from letters, sheep stealing and horse stealing.

Until 1868 executions were great public spectacles with towns like Edinburgh, Glasgow, Aberdeen, Ayr, Cupar, Dundee, Dumfries and Stirling, taking on a carnival atmosphere on such occasions.

Drama and excitement were always present; justice frequently poetic, in the literal sense, as the following street ballad illustrates. It described the farewell of a convicted murderer at Edinburgh:-

Great was the throng to see him hung
For crimes that were so vile.
To Edinburgh upon that day
They tramped for many a mile.
They led him out all clad in black —
Black coat and vest so white —
A mocking smile was on his lips,
He wore a nosegay bright".

In Glasgow two lovers convicted of murder 'married' on the scaffold before the hangman despatched them.

On another occasion 750 constables were drafted in to maintain order at the execution of a doctor who had murdered his wife and mother-in-law.

This was the city's last public hanging.

A newspaper reporter present wrote: "After the bolt was drawn he shrugged his shoulders more than half a dozen times, his head shook, and the whole body trembled."

In Edinburgh there was a riot when a man showed signs of life after the execution. Order was restored and the process repeated an hour later.

For years the Rob Roy tartan was shunned by women the length and breadth of Scotland after a city woman appeared on the scaffold clad in a Rob Roy shawl.

There were many other aspects to these occasions which would strike us today as singularly bizarre.

The condemned man or woman was often brought to the scaffold in an open cart — sitting atop their own coffin.

The hangman had to wear a disguise for fear of reprisals from the crowd who could often turn violent especially if it was felt that a miscarriage of justice was taking place.

After the event bodies were usually transported to Edinburgh Medical School for dissection and study by students.

AS often as not when petitions were launched to try and have the death sentence set aside it was the jurors who were first to sign!

Every detail of the convicted person's last hours was eagerly gleaned from the newspapers.

Joseph Bell who murdered a baker's vanman in Perthshire asked the minister to deliver books to his death cell. He then composed poems to his nearest and dearest on the morning of his execution and wrote them on the inside title pages.

The message received by his parents read:-

"Dear Father and Mother, it's the 12th of May;
I wrote these lines for you today;
Sad news they will have to tell,
About our parting, Joseph Bell.
In remembrance of me pray keep this book,
With earnest eyes do on it look,
For this day we must take farewell.
Your loving son, Joseph Bell".

T.M.Tod in his introduction to the original edition wrote: "This book purposes to be little more than a record of some criminal trials and executions in Scotland over a century.

"A brief résumé of the evidence is given in several of the important trials, while notes are also added.

"A number of cases which deserve little or no public notice are included, mainly because capital convictions were returned.

"The information has been mostly gleaned from personal perusal of newspapers, as relaxation in country life during the winter evenings throughout a long period of years".

Mr Tod tells how teenager Robert Smith, who had brutally murdered a nine-year-old girl was the last man to be publicly executed in Scotland on May 12, 1868.

The first private execution took place within the walls of the County Prison, Perth, on Tuesday, October 4, 1870.

He was present at one trial when the death penalty was passed and wrote: "It seemed almost hours, although it could only be the matter of several minutes, before the Clerk of the Court had written out the death sentence on the Court Record.

"A pin could almost be heard to drop; there is no sound in the hushed Court except the scratching pen of the Clerk hurrying over the old-world formula in the leather-bound book of doom.

"The Clerk has finished writing, and the macer hands the book to his Lordship who, assuming the black cap, in clear and distinct tones reads out the sentence.

"The tension is over, the prisoner is removed below, and the crowd slowly disperses.

"Those who have witnessed such a scene will probably remember it to their dying day.

"It is horribly fascinating, hideously impressive and dramatic."

Elsewhere in these pages Mr Tod tells of the judge who would sink to his knees in prayer when a jury retired in a capital case.

Although many serious homicide cases passed through this learned fellow's hands during 20 years on the bench the capital verdict was not returned in a single instance.

He recalls the case of the pregnant wife who escaped execution — but only until her baby was born.

Find out what happened to 22 men who stood before a judge at Stirling facing a sentence of death, followed by their heads being chopped off and their bodies quartered ...

...About murder and piracy on the high seas, the division of a treasure in Spanish coins on a Barra beach and subsequent execution of the culprits on the Sands of Leith ...

...The Glasgow Dynamiters — 10 men charged with blowing up a gasometer at Tradestown containing 3,500 cubic feet of gas and attempting to blow up the canal bridge at Possil Park ...

...The rat catcher who stole an earl's corpse from its lead coffin in the family vault ...

...And some remarkable and complex cases which came before the Scottish courts and in which juries returned not proven verdicts.

★ Please note that the last line on page 120 should read:-
'gun. A 12-bore wad covered in blood which had been found'...
The phrase 12-bore gun was used in error in the original edition. Three black and white photographs showing the scene of the Blairgowrie murder, 1866; Ardlamont House and scene of tragedy at Ardlamont have not been included in this edition. Readers are reminded that any topical references by the author should be taken as relating to the conditions at the time of writing.

BIBLIOGRAPHIC NOTE

'The Scots Black Kalendar' was first published at Perth in 1938 by Munro and Scott. We would like to thank them and Mr Tod's successor at West Brackley, Kinross, Mr W Nelson, for their assistance in making this new edition possible.
Published by Lang Syne Publishers Ltd., Newtongrange, Midlothian in 1985 and printed by Waterside Printers, Old School, Blanefield, Stirlingshire.
©Lang Syne Publishers Ltd. and W.Nelson for T.M.Tod.
ISBN: 0 946264 93 7

The Scots Black Kalendar.

1800.

May 28. Peter Greig hanged at Glasgow for hamesucken.

[This term, which is peculiar to Scots law, is now nearly obsolete and is constituted by committing great violence upon one in his dwelling-house. Previous to 1887 this was a capital offence. Charges of such a nature now usually come under the term " assault."]

Thomas Urquhart, postmaster, Orkney, hanged at Edinburgh for opening letters and taking out money.

[Orkney and Shetland not being on any circuit, cases from those islands come before the High Court at Edinburgh.]

1802.

February 10. Andrew Lawrie, letter carrier, hanged at Edinburgh for theft of money from letters.

1806.

April 29. At Inverness Circuit Court, before Lord Meadowbank, Nicholas Ross and John M'Pherson, styled as " out-pensioners " of Chelsea Hospital, were found guilty of fraud. They were ordained to stand in the pillory with a label on their breasts bearing the following inscription:—" For defrauding their King and Master by false certificates "; thereafter to be banished from Scotland throughout all the days of their lives.

May 9. Perth Circuit Court was opened on this date. Three capital convictions were recorded during the sittings.

John Westwater, a flax dresser from Kinghorn, was convicted of the murder of a fellow workman. He was hanged at Kinghorn on Saturday, 21st June.

B

Margaret Cunningham or Masson, widow of John Masson, Pathhead, Kirkcaldy, and John Skinner, were charged with the murder of her husband by administering arsenic. Skinner, who had absconded, had sentence of fugitation passed upon him. Mrs. Masson was found guilty, but sentence was delayed, as her counsel said that she was *enciente*.

Donald M'Craw, a merchant in Perth, was found guilty of the murder of a little girl. M'Craw was hanged at Perth on the 11th July.

[The case of Mrs. Masson subsequently came before the High Court at Edinburgh, when a jury of midwives certified that she was pregnant. Sentence was therefore postponed for five months. She appeared again before the Court in November with the child in her arms, when sentence of death was passed. This sentence was duly carried out on the 7th January. Clemency might surely have been extended to this unfortunate woman, as her companion in crime had escaped from being brought to trial.]

1807.

January 21. Smith and Stevenson hanged at Edinburgh for horse stealing.

September 21. At Inveraray Circuit Court, before Lord Craig, Peter M'Dougal, alias M'Laggan, was convicted of the murder of his wife by throwing her into the River Etive, near Kingshouse Inn, in December. The prisoner was sentenced to be hanged at Inveraray on the 16th November. A respite was, however, granted for fourteen days, but on the 28th November the condemned man was taken in a cart, sitting on the top of his coffin, from Inveraray Jail to the Craigs, a mile distant from the town, where he paid the penalty. "Tam" Young, the Glasgow hangman, officiated. The body was handed over to Mr. John Anderson, surgeon in Inveraray, for the purpose of dissection.

[This was the last instance of the infliction of the capital sentence in the annals of the quaint old circuit town.]

September 23. Archibald Begg, a resurrectionist who had been banished from Scotland, was whipped through the streets of Edinburgh for returning before his term had expired.

1810.

September 27. At Inverness Circuit Court, before the Lord Justice Clerk (Hope), Alexander Gillan (19) was convicted of murder and rape. Gillan was hanged on the 14th November where the tragedy was enacted, and his body, pursuant to the sentence, afterwards hung in chains. After Gillan's remains had hung for some time they were taken down and buried, chains and all, at the foot of the scaffold.

1811.

June 7. George Watson hanged at Ayr for horse-stealing.

October 26. Thomas M'Nair hanged at Falkirk for robbery.

1813.

December 29. Christina Sinclair, from Orkney, hanged at Edinburgh for child murder.

1815.

January 25. Two Irishmen, Kelly and O'Neil, were hanged at Braidburn, Edinburgh, for highway robbery committed there. The procession left the Tolbooth at one o'clock in the afternoon in the following order:—Police Constables, High Constables—three and three—Magistrates of the City, the Rev. Dr. Brunton of the Tron Church, two Roman Catholic Priests, and the Lieutenant of Police. Then came the cart with the condemned men and the hangman, surrounded by the City Guard. The Sheriff took over command at Main Point, where the city then terminated, and led the procession on horseback, accompanied by a large retinue of officials. After the sentence was carried out at three o'clock, the bodies were taken back under escort and buried in Greyfriars Churchyard.

[Just where Braid Road is joined by Comiston Terrace, two square stones lying level with the roadway mark the spot where the scaffold was erected.]

1817.

January 20. John Larg, James Mitchell, and Alexander Steel, were capitally convicted at Edinburgh for housebreaking and robbery at Friarton Toll Bar, Perth, on the 12th-13th November. When the men were at first refused admission they threatened to set the cottage on fire or discharge a pistol through the window. The toll-keeper was in such fear of his life that he opened the door, when the trio took all the money they could find, amounting to about eight shillings. The men were hanged at Perth on the 28th February.

May 26. Before the High Court of Justiciary at Edinburgh, a Universalist preacher named Neil Douglas was charged with sedition. Douglas was an old man of independent means, who had no church of his own but rented the Andersonian Institute in Glasgow for services on Sundays. He cherished the utmost hatred against King George III., and his prodigal son, as he called the Prince Regent. It was announced that Douglas was to lecture one Sunday afternoon on the Prophecies of Daniel*: such large crowds flocked to his meeting-place that the little hall could have been filled twice over. In the course of his lecture he drew a parallel between the King and Nebuchadnezzar, King of Babylon, remarking that they were both noted for infidelity and corruption. He also denounced the Prince Regent as a poor infatuated creature, over head and ears in love with Bacchus. Douglas was arrested shortly after the service. The principal witnesses for the Crown were two Officers sent by the Magistrates to take note of what Douglas had said. The men were so severely cross-examined by Jeffrey, who appeared for the defence, that the charge was withdrawn. The Lord Justice Clerk who presided took the opportunity of cautioning Douglas to be more careful of his language in future.

July 18 and 23. Before the High Court of Justiciary at Edinburgh, Andrew M'Kinley, a weaver and a prominent Radical reformer at Glasgow, described as "presently a State prisoner in Edinburgh Castle," was charged with high treason. M'Kinley

---

* Daniel, chap. v., verses 7-23.

was gratuitously defended by the most celebrated pleaders of his day, Moncreiff, Jeffrey, and Cockburn. The proceedings were, however, brought to an abrupt conclusion by a Crown witness named Campbell (also a State prisoner), who deposed that Mr. Drummond, Advocate-Depute, had offered him a reward to secure a conviction against M'Kinley.

[Happily this is the last instance where the Crown endeavoured to secure a conviction by bribery.]

September 5. Before the High Court of Justiciary, Edinburgh, three Irish labourers, named Bernard and Hugh M'Ilrogue and Patrick M'Crostal, were sentenced to death for housebreaking, robbery and assault, committed at the house of Mr. Morris, farmer, Everton, near Greenock. They bound Mr. Morris, robbed the house, and then committed an assault upon his sister-in-law and the maidservant. The men were hanged at Greenock on the 10th October. Upwards of 10,000 spectators were present.

September 11. At Ayr Circuit Court, William Robertson and Joseph Cairns were sentenced to death for robbery and theft. Margaret Crossan (50), a native of Ireland, received a similar sentence for fire-raising at Carsegowan, Wigton, in May last, whereby the greater part of the farm steading was destroyed, as well as twelve cows, a bull, and three calves. The act was committed out of malice against the proprietor, who had threatened to put her out of her house. Crossan was hanged at Ayr, along with the two men, on the 17th October—the only instance of a triple execution in the town.

William Hamilton was at the same Circuit sentenced to death for housebreaking. The sentence, fixed also to be carried out on the 17th October, was, however, commuted.

1818.

April 25. Before the High Court of Justiciary at Edinburgh, two boys, Mair and Aitchison, both under sixteen years of age, were sentenced to death for housebreaking at Coates Crescent, Edinburgh. The youths cried most piteously when desired to stand up, and fell down below the bar. They were subsequently supported by police officers when Lord Hermand passed sentence.

June 5. John Ritchie (17), hanged at Aberdeen for sheep stealing at Gordon Castle Policies. There were no previous convictions, and strenuous efforts were made to secure a reprieve. This proved unsuccessful, as sheep stealing was prevalent in the district and the number stolen was thirty.

October 3. At Glasgow Circuit Court, Matthew Clydesdale, a miner from the Middle Ward of Lanarkshire, was found guilty of murder. He was sentenced to be hanged on the 4th November, while the judges, Lords Gillies and Succoth, adjudged that the body be publicly dissected and anatomised by Professor Jeffrey, of Glasgow University. When "Tam" Young, "the finisher of the law" in the city, had done his duty, the body was conveyed to the College. A remarkable scene then ensued. Clydesdale was brought back to life again by a galvanic shock, and stood up and faced the astonished students and the professor. The latter was equal to the occasion, for, taking out a lancet he plunged it into the jugular vein and the man fell on the floor, as it has been described, "like a slaughtered ox on the blow of a butcher." The proceedings caused a great sensation in the city, and in order to guard against a repetition of such a gruesome occurrence, this was the last order for dissection made by the Circuit judges at Glasgow.

[It is believed if the lancet had not been used this would probably have been another case like the noteworthy one of "Half-hangit" Margaret Dickson in 1724. After being hanged at Edinburgh for concealment of pregnancy, she was brought back to life again in her coffin by the jolting of the cart over the rough stones at Peffermill on the way to the burial at Inveresk Churchyard. She subsequently married and had children.]

November 6. John Barnet, hanged at Aberdeen for a number of thefts by housebreaking at Peterhead. His body was taken out to sea and put overboard, but a few days later it was cast ashore at the mouth of the Don, when it was handed over for the purpose of dissection. He was convicted at the Autumn Court in Aberdeen.

December 30. Robert Johnstone (23), who had been sentenced to death by the High Court at Edinburgh, was hanged in the city on this date, amidst the most horrible and unparalleled scene which has ever taken place at an execution. When the drop fell at three o'clock in the afternoon Johnstone was found to be alive, although insensible. The dense crowd which surrounded the scaffold were awe stricken when it was found the man was not dead. Quick action was taken, and someone with a knife in hand jumped on to the scaffold and cut the rope. He was followed by a lame man with a crutch, and then a general rush ensued, the authorities being powerless. Bailie Pattison, surrounded by a strong body of police, marched to the Castle to summon military assistance, but while proceeding up the Lawnmarket they came in contact with a section of the crowd, carrying the almost lifeless body of Johnstone. This caused the bearers to change their course and they turned down the High Street. Opposite the Police Office they encountered a force of constables who had now arrived, and after a sharp encounter the crowd fled, leaving their burden on the street. The constables carried Johnstone into the Police Office until the arrival of a detachment of the 88th Regiment, followed by another from the Castle under Major Graham. The streets were now cleared by the military, and order was restored. Johnstone was then carried to the scaffold and finally launched into eternity one hour after the rescue.

Whether the reanimation of Johnstone was complete or only partial was never satisfactorily ascertained. The military remained on guard until all the dismal paraphernalia were removed and the crowd was dispersed. The cause of the dreadful affair was some defect in the construction of the scaffold, which was a new one. When the bolt was drawn Johnstone was seen to be standing on his tip-toes.

On the 25th January of the following year, the Lord Advocate presented precognitions to the High Court regarding the attempt to carry off the body of the criminal. He reported that after investigation the authorities had failed to discover the persons principally concerned in the riot. There was also no ground for taking action against the Magistrates for failing in their duty. The Lord Justice-Clerk who presided approved of the course the Lord Advocate had taken, and moved the Court to return the

precognition unopened, as after the explanation there was no point
to decide. This became the finding of the Court.

[Mr. Horace Bleakley, in his "Hangmen of England,"
mentions that the official who bungled was one John Foster, who
was dismissed from office after the execution by the Magistrates
of Edinburgh.]

1819.

April 7. Quintuple execution at Glasgow. Robert M'Kinglay,
Hunter Guthrie, John Forbes, William Buchanan, and Alexander
Robertson, hanged at Glasgow for housebreaking.

July 19 and 20. Before the High Court of Justiciary at
Edinburgh, Ralph Woodness and Richard Smith were charged
with housebreaking and theft of goods to the value of £350 at
Linlithgow. Woodness was capitally convicted, but the charge
against his companion was found not proven. Woodness was
hanged at Linlithgow on Friday, 27th August.

August 11. James Whiteford hanged at Edinburgh for hamesucken at Hopetoun Toll Bar, Linlithgow. He had assaulted the
toll-keeper and his daughter, presented a revolver at the former
and compelled him to open a chest which contained money, and
did steal it.

November 17. John Buchanan hanged at Glasgow for murder.
He had been twitted by a companion some time previous to the
tragedy that he would yet die "with his face to the Monument."
This was equivalent to saying he would be hanged in front of the
centre piazzas at the Jail, which faces the Nelson Monument on
the Green. Buchanan swore that would never happen, and he
kept his word, for he astonished the hangman by turning round
with his face to the side.

November 28. Bryce Judd and Thomas Clapperton capitally
convicted before the High Court of Justiciary at Edinburgh for
hamesucken and stouthrief. They broke into a house near
Harvieston, Gorebridge, and stole a bank receipt for £263, three
blankets, and a can of butter. The men told the occupants of the
house that if they watched which way they went a gun would be
fired at them. The prisoners were subsequently apprehended at

Tranent. They paid the full penalty at Edinburgh on the 5th January.

1820.

The Radical Rising and its Consequences

On Sunday, 1st April, a treasonable address was posted throughout Glasgow calling on the weavers to cease work. The address began:—" Friends and countrymen, raised from that state in which we have been sunk for so many years, we are at length compelled by the extremity of our sufferings and the contempt heaped upon our Petition for Redress to assert our rights at the hazard of our lives." In glowing language, a perfect " Fiery Cross," the address called the country to arms, in the true Irish sense, " agin the Government," and concluded with the words:— " By order of the Committee of Organisation for forming a Provisional Government, Glasgow, 1st April, 1820."

The discontent had arisen through a large number of handloom weavers being in a state of starvation. The agitators aimed at a reform in their interests by the House of Commons and the repeal of the Corn Laws. Great alarm prevailed in the city, and the Magistrates issued a proclamation ordering all shops to be closed by 6 p.m., and requesting citizens to be in their houses an hour later, while strangers were enjoined to withdraw from the city by 7 p.m. The proclamation set forth " that the military would be employed in the most decisive manner against all those coming forward to aid in rebellion."

Dr. Chalmers, then minister of St. John's, Glasgow, made earnest supplication to counteract " the state of civil war now approaching in this city." Military guarded the principal buildings, while artillery held the bridges over the Clyde. Disorder, however, continued to reign, but the authorities were active and many arrests were made. The Jail was so full that a number of prisoners were escorted to Greenock Prison by the Port-Glasgow Volunteers. On the return journey the Volunteers were attacked by a mob, but they immediately opened fire, four of the rioters being killed.

A meeting of Reformers was convened at Gadshill, near Glasgow, when one, Andrew Hardie, took a prominent part. It was there reported that risings had taken place all over England and that the mail coaches had been stopped. Under the leadership of Hardie, at twelve midnight, after the meeting, about forty persons marched off, armed with guns and pikes, gathering forces as they went. Their plan was to secure sufficient followers within a few days' march, and then join forces with others who were supposed to take possession of Glasgow. They proceeded to Condorrat and on to Castlecary. Here the Reformers divided forces, the second being in command of John Baird. Various houses were plundered in search of arms, and a private of the Hussars was held up. He was, however, allowed to go when he said that their political principles were good. On reaching head-quarters, the Hussar reported his experience, and a force of Hussars and Yeomanry were sent out. The combined rebel divisions met the Crown forces at Bonnymuir, near Falkirk. After a sharp skirmish, in which Hardie attempted to shoot the Officer in charge of the Hussars, the rebels were routed. Eighteen persons were taken prisoner, including Hardie. One was left wounded on the field, while a considerable number fled. Five muskets, two pistols, sixteen pikes, one hay fork, one shaft, and a quantity of ball cartridges were taken possession of by the troops.

A weaver named James Wilson, of Strathaven, was also a prominent Reformer, and meetings were held in his house. Hearing that Glasgow was in revolt, Wilson gathered together a number of supporters, whom he had compelled by threats of death to join him or to hand over their firearms. By the same means he forced shopkeepers to provide him with gunpowder and shot. The party, now armed with guns and pikes, proceeded in marching order in the direction of Glasgow. Prominent in the procession was a flag with the words, "Scotland Free or a Desert." Wilson brought up the rear with a drawn sword in his hand. On reaching Kilbride, seven miles distant, they were informed that Glasgow was quiet, and that the attempted insurrection had not been successful. This war-like little party at once disbanded. Some returned to their homes, while others fled. Wilson was arrested in his own house the same evening.

Such is a brief description of the salient points of the rising. The Government took a serious view of the situation, and decided to arraign all the principal prisoners under a charge of high treason. Since the Union in 1707, the English procedure is followed in trials of this class, and Mr. Serjeant Hullock, of the English Bar, was retained to aid the Scots Law Officers. His retaining fee was said to be 2,000 guineas. Lord Chief Baron Shepherd was also sent down to assist the Scots Lords of Session. The insurgents captured at Bonnymuir had been confined in Edinburgh Castle as State prisoners, but they were removed to Stirling Castle two days previous to the opening of the trial.

This was a Commission of Oyer and Termiher,* which opened at Stirling on the 23rd June. The Lords of the Commission arrived in the town on the 22nd June. They were met at St. Ninians by the Provost and Magistrates, who escorted them to the Red Lion Inn. In the words of the poet, truly " The season of Oyer and Terminer had come." Great interest was manifested in the trials, and the newspaper chronicles that " the town is crowded to excess and scarcely any accommodation remains for man or beast."

June 23 and 24. The Special Commission Court was held on this date before Lord President Hope, Lord Justice-Clerk Boyle, Lord Chief Baron Shepherd of the English Bench, Lord Chief Commissioner Adam of the Jury Court, Lord Hermand and Lord Gillies. The proceedings were held in the Court House in Broad. Street. (This room was, until a few years ago, still used for the Burgh Police Court). The Commission having been duly constituted by prayer from a minister, and " fenced " by proclamation by the crier, Mr. Knapp, of London, was sworn by the Lord President as Clerk of Court. Two Commissions were intimated, one in Latin and the other in English, and the Lords directed Mr. Knapp to read the English Commission. Mr. James Rae, of Parliament Square, Edinburgh, was appointed Crier of Court, and two Macers were attached to the Tribunal. A Grand Jury was then empanelled, with the Hon. George Abercromby as foreman. A long oath was administered to him, and the remainder of the jury, twenty-two in number, were sworn in four at a time.

The Lord President, in his charge to the grand jury, said that the only previous charges of treason in Scotland since the Union

---

* Oyer and Terminer—" Oyer " is French, to hear, and " Terminer," to conclude—To hear and conclude a Commission.

in 1707 were the cases of Watt and Downie in 1794. His Lordship
explained that the old Scots law of treason had now given place
to that of England, founded in the days of Edward III. True bills
were returned against Andrew Hardie, John Baird, and sixteen
others. The prosecution was in the hands of the Lord Advocate,
Sir William Rae, the Solicitor-General Wedderburn, Mr. Serjeant
Hulloch, Mr. Drummond, Mr. Maconochie, and Mr. Hope,
Advocates-Depute. Mr. Jeffrey and Mr. Grant were assigned as
counsel for the defendants.

The Court met again the following day, when other charges
were considered by the grand jury against persons not in custody,
and true bills were also returned. The charges against the
defendants were four in number. The first charge in the indictment contained no fewer than nineteen overt* acts; second, levying
war; third, compassing and intending to depose the King; and
fourth, compassing to levy war against the King in order to compel
him to change his measures. Pleas of not guilty were tendered,
and the trial of Andrew Hardie was adjourned until the 13th July.
After evidence had been led, following the English procedure, Mr.
Jeffrey for the defence addressed the jury first, and the Solicitor-
General replied. Hardie was found guilty. (Following again the
English custom, the verdict of the jury had to be unanimous).
John Baird, on the 15th July, was found guilty on the second
charge only, while others who had been present at Bonnymuir,
and also in connection with a case from Camelon, withdrew their
plea of not guilty and admitted the crimes. The Lord Advocate,
on the 4th August, intimated that justice had been done, as
twenty-two men were awaiting sentence, and he would consent
to the acquittal of the remainder of the defendants.

The Lord Advocate then moved for sentence against the twenty-
two men who were put to the bar. They were each asked if they
had anything to say " why judgment to die according to law should
not be pronounced against them." There was no reply, and each
bowed to the Court. The Lord President, in his opening address,
said: " Andrew Hardie, John Baird, James Clelland, Thomas
M'Culloch, Benjamin Moir, Allen Marchie, Alexander Latimer,
Alexander Johnstone, Andrew Whyte, David Thomson, James

---

*An English Law term—An open act which must be clearly proved.

Whyte, William Clackson, Thomas Pink, Robert Gray, Alexander Hart, John Barr, William Smith, Thomas M'Farlane, John Anderson, William Crawford, John M'Millan and Andrew Dawson, you present the melancholy spectacle of two-and-twenty subjects of this country who have forfeited their lives to its justice, a spectacle, I believe, unexampled in the history of this country; such at least I have never witnessed, and I trust to God never shall I witness again." His Lordship concluded a long and impressive address by saying: "To you, Andrew Hardie and John Baird, I can hold out little or no hope of mercy, as you were selected as the leaders of that band in which you were associated. To the others clemency might be extended, but I counsel you to prepare for the worst." The Lord President passed sentence in these words: "The sentence of the law is that you and each of you be taken to the place of execution, there to be hanged by the neck until you are dead, and afterwards your head severed from your body and your body divided into four quarters, to be disposed of as His Majesty may direct. And may God in His infinite goodness have mercy on your souls. I have only to intimate now that a warrant will be signed by this Court for your execution on Friday, the 8th day of September."

The warrant for the execution, after detailing the circumstances in which the Commission had met, fixed the carrying out of the sentence between the hours of 12 o'clock noon and 4 o'clock in the afternoon. It was signed: "C. Hope, S. Shepherd, and D. Monypenny" (Lord Pitmilly). The warrant was addressed to: "The Sheriff-Depute, his Substitute, the Provost and Magistrates of Stirling, and all others whom it may concern."

The prisoners were then removed to Stirling Castle. A reprieve was subsequently granted in the case of twenty of the men, who were afterwards transported, but the law was allowed to take its course in the case of Hardie and Baird. On the 8th September, a touching farewell was taken between them and their fellow-prisoners through a cell window. A short religious service was held for the condemned men. The first four verses of the 51st Paraphrase were sung, while the 15th chapter of 1st Corinthians was read. Shortly before the time fixed for the execution, two o'clock, the men were taken outside the Castle gate to the hurdle which was waiting. Guarded by military, the procession set out for Broad Street, where the scaffold had been erected opposite the Courthouse. A great concourse of people thronged the whole route; the crowd around the scaffold was particularly dense, but a troop of the 7th Dragoon Guards and the 15th Regiment of Foot held the ground. Both Hardie and Baird, according to the custom of the time, addressed the multitude from the scaffold. The bolt was then drawn, and pursuant to the sentence, half-an-hour later the hangman, who wore a black domino mask, cut off the heads with an axe. At this first he shouted: "This is the head of a traitor," and, the other, "This is the head of another traitor." The hangman subsequently flung the heads down to the black coffins underneath, amidst the shrieks and groans of the spectators. The quartering, by order of His Majesty, was dispensed with. Slowly the great crowd began to disperse, and so terminated the last execution in Scotland for high treason.

Excellent order was maintained by the Sheriff of Stirlingshire (Macdonald of Staffa), and the Magistrates of Stirling.

[It may be added that the abolition of the Forfeiture Act* of 1870 in England annulled the barbaric judgment which follows a conviction for high treason; but in Scotland to-day the penalty is just as severe and even revolting as when the strife of parties involved the fate of the dynasty, a conviction still demands the penalty of being hanged, drawn and quartered in addition to corruption of blood and forfeiture of all goods. The Private Execution Act of 1868 does not apply in Scotland to this high crime, and unless otherwise directed the persons must suffer death in public. Such an exhibition would not be permitted, and the final scene would now take place behind prison walls. In the Smith Institute, Stirling, some grim reminders of the execution can still be seen. There is the axe, as well as the cloak of sackcloth with the mask which covered the hangman, who was never identified. When the trials took place, and indeed up to the death of the Duke of Montrose in 1836, the office of Lord Justice-General of Scotland was always held by a nobleman, but at his death the office was combined with that of the Lord President of the Court of Session. This, therefore, accounts for

---

*54 Geo. III., C 146.

Lord President Hope, who presided, being styled Lord President instead of Lord Justice-General.]

July 24. A Special Commission Court of Oyer and Terminer, which had been opened in Glasgow in June, with the same judges and officials as at Stirling, passed sentence on this date on James Wilson (60), a weaver from Strathaven. He had been found guilty of compassing to levy war against the King to compel him to change his measures. Wilson was recommended to the clemency of the Crown. Charges against other defendants were withdrawn. James Wilson was then put to the bar.

The Lord President, in a long address in passing sentence, described the prisoner as "a miserable and sinful creature, about perhaps shortly to appear at the mercy seat of Almighty God, where you must answer not only for this crime of which you have been convicted, but for all the sins and vices of your past life." Wilson was ordained to be hanged, drawn and quartered at Glasgow, on Wednesday, 30th August. Strenuous efforts were made on behalf of the unfortunate man that mercy might be extended to him, but the Government decided that an example must be made. Accordingly Wilson paid the penalty in front of the Justiciary Buildings, at the foot of the Saltmarket, Glasgow. Strong detachments of the 3rd Dragoon Guards, the 38th Regiment, and the Rifle Brigade were present. Dressed in white prison clothes draped with black, Wilson was brought up from the "Iron Room" to the Justiciary Court, where a short religious service was held. Wilson, who was quite calm and collected, invited those present to join with him in singing several verses of the 51st Psalm. The hurdle was then brought along the passage. It was accompanied by "Tam" Young, the hangman. His face was covered with a black mask, while he carried a gleaming axe and straps in his hand. Wilson then took his seat on the hurdle, which was drawn outside and round by the south side of the building to the scaffold. This had been erected on its usual stance facing the Green.

Executions, of course, always drew a large gathering, but on this occasion 20,000 persons were present. During a stampede of the crowd, when it was believed the military were to charge,

many persons fell into the Molendinar Burn. Wilson, who was
of venerable appearance, on mounting the scaffold and viewing
the seething mass of heads in front of him, exclaimed to the
executioner, "Did ye ever see sic a crood?" "Oh, aye, I've seen
as big a crood as that afore," replied Tam.

The noose was then adjusted and the bolt drawn. Subsequently, the body was lifted on to the scaffold and laid on a black
board. One blow from the axe was sufficient, and holding up the
head, Tam uttered the words: "Behold the head of a traitor."
Cries of "Shame!" and "Murder!" were heard above the din.
As the quartering was dispensed with, the mangled remains were
placed in a black coffin which had been lying in full view of the
spectators, and was buried in the Cathedral Burying Ground. But
at dead of night Wilson's daughter and niece, along with some
friends who had come to Glasgow for the execution, lifted the body
and conveyed it in a cart to Strathaven for burial in Wilson's
own garden.

[Wilson, who believed he was a patriot for his country, was
no doubt a vain, misguided old man, who did not realise the
serious position in which others had placed him. He acquired
the soubriquet of "Pearley Wilson," from the fact that he
invented the "purl stitch." His house has long been removed,
but a suitable monument has been erected in Strathaven to his
memory. The following is the inscription: "1846. Erected by
public subscription in affectionate memory of James Wilson, a
patriotic Scotsman, who suffered death at Glasgow, 30th August,
1820, for enunciating those principles of progress and reform by
the adoption of which Great Britain has secured domestic peace,
and consolidated her power among the nations. Born at Strathaven, 5th September, 1760." It is said that the sword which was
carried by Wilson now belongs to Councillor John S. Clark, of
Maryhill.]

June 29 and July 12. Special Commission Courts of Oyer and
Terminer were also held in Dumbarton Church, St. George's
Parish Church, Paisley, and in Ayr Parish Church, but verdicts
of not guilty were returned, except in the case of Thomas Mackay
at the last-named place. The Lord Justice-Clerk who presided

sentenced Mackay to be hanged, drawn and quartered, on the 15th September, but the sentence was commuted.

[This was the last instance of a Commission of Oyer and Terminer being issued in Scotland. It is unusual to have criminal proceedings taking place in Church, but this course had to be adopted for want of suitable accommodation.]

June 19. Before the High Court of Justiciary at Edinburgh, James Mackoull, a well-known London thief, was found guilty of robbing the Paisley Union Bank, Ingram Street, Glasgow, of £20,000 on the 13th July, 1811. Mackoull had been arrested in London and brought to Glasgow in April, 1812, but as there was not sufficient evidence for the case to go to trial, and the prisoner having "run his letters,"* he was liberated in July. On landing at Leith, on the 4th March, 1813, he was once more arrested, but again liberated. Mackoull subsequently brought an action in the Court of Session against the Bank for the recovery of £1,000 found in his possession when arrested. He also brought an action against Bailie Johnstone, Edinburgh, and the Procurator-Fiscal, for damages. The Bank at this turn of events now employed a celebrated detective, Mr. Denovan, the Bow Street runner, to endeavour to secure fresh evidence to connect Mackoull with the robbery. A number of witnesses were brought from England, who testified that the prisoner and two other companions posted to Edinburgh from London a short time before the robbery in 1811. The evidence was almost purely circumstantial, but a waiter at an inn at Barnett deponed that he recognised the prisoner as the man who was sitting in a room there, dividing out a large quantity of Scotch bank notes with two friends. Mackoull, although sentenced to death, was however not to suffer death by the hangman. A respite was granted both in August and in September. Latterly he became insane, and died in the Calton Jail, Edinburgh, on the 22nd December.

[It is generally believed that this notorious villain was also responsible for the murder of Begbie, the British Linen Company's Bank porter, who was robbed of £4,392 in notes at Tweeddale Court, Edinburgh, on the 13th November, 1806. A reward of 500 guineas

---

*An old Act of 1701, by which a person in custody must be brought to trial within a reasonable period.

C

was offered to secure a conviction, but this was unsuccessful. Some of the lost bank notes were discovered in the Bellevue district in August, 1807. The Bank rewarded the finders with £200.]

October 23. Edward M'Rory hanged at Dumfries for assault and robbery at Carse of Slaiks, between Gatehouse and Creetown. He was convicted at the Circuit, and to the last maintained he was innocent.

November 8. Four men—Grant, Crosbie, Connor, and M'Colgan—hanged at Glasgow for housebreaking.

1821.

June 6. James Gordon hanged at Dumfries for the murder of John Elliot, a young pedlar, near Upper Cassock, Eskdalemuir, in November last. Gordon, who was an Irishman, made the acquaintance of Elliot at a farm in Canonbie Parish, where they spent the night. On the pretence that Gordon knew a short cut across the hills to Moffat, he induced Elliot to accompany him. The body of the man was found with many wounds in his head, while his pedlar's pack had been rifled. Suspicion rested upon the Irishman, who had disappeared. A description of the wanted man was published in the " Dumfries Courier," but several months passed and still there was no trace of the suspect, who seemed to have vanished into space.

Then a curious, and what might be described as an unprecedented occurrence, took place, which bears out the adage, " Murder will out." A traveller in an hotel at Nairn, in order to pass the time on a wet day, took up an old copy of the Dumfries paper containing the description of Gordon. After reading it, he turned his eyes across the street, and there, standing before him, was a man who answered the description in almost every detail. The traveller immediately accosted the man, who was so taken by surprise when asked if he was Gordon that he admitted he was. The police were called and Gordon was arrested. He was removed to Dumfries, and convicted at the Spring Circuit.

July 18. David Haggart (18), a notorious gaol-breaker and murderer, hanged at Edinburgh. While confined in Dumfries Jail

...? secreted a stone, which he put into a bag. When the turnkey, named Warren, brought Haggart some food to the cell, the prisoner struck him over the head with the bag, with fatal effect. Haggart then made his escape. On the scaffold he expressed great contrition, and earnestly enjoined the crowd to avoid heinous crimes, and pay attention to the Bible.

[Cockburn, who defended him, said there was never a riper scoundrel, a more perfect and inveterate miscreant, in all the darker walks of crime.]

September 19. At Perth Circuit Court, before the Lord Justice-Clerk (Boyle) and Lord Pitmilly, Margaret Tyndall or Shuttleworth (36) was charged with the murder of her husband, a vintner, at Montrose. She pleaded not guilty. The jury who were empanelled were mostly composed of landed proprietors, and included such well-known names as Smythe of Methven, Belshes of Invermay, Keir of Huntingtower, Oswald of Dunnikeir (foreman), Cathcart of Pitcairlie, and Briggs of Strathairlie. Evidence was led which was to the effect that the deceased was found dead in a passage of the house with his head horribly mutilated. A blood-stained poker was found in the room where Mrs. Shuttleworth had been asleep. Suspicion from the first rested upon the prisoner owing to the fact that all the windows and doors were found fastened from the inside.

Among the witnesses was a servant girl, who said the couple lived happily together when they were sober, but her mistress was much addicted to drink. On the evening in question she had put her to bed much intoxicated, and went out to attend a wake, leaving the deceased, who was also under the influence of drink, in another room. A unanimous verdict of guilty—or "all in one voice," as the phraseology of the record termed it—was returned. Sentence of death was passed, to be carried out at Montrose on the 2nd November, between the hours of 2 and 4 o'clock in the afternoon. Lord Pitmilly, in passing sentence, concurred with the verdict of the "intelligent jury." A petition was forwarded to the Home Secretary praying for a respite, in order that fuller inquiries might be made. The petition set forth that the evidence was entirely circumstantial; there was no motive, the prisoner was intoxicated when put to bed, she was the first to give the alarm, and lastly, behaved as a person unconscious of guilt would have done. A respite for one month was subsequently granted.

Meantime the Sheriff examined witnesses, but nothing seems to have transpired in favour of the prisoner. A legal doubt, however, arose, whether the respite was for a lunar or calendar month. This point was remitted to twelve judges in England, when it was determined that an extension of five days should be granted. Accordingly, on the 7th December, Mrs. Shuttleworth suffered the full penalty at Montrose, still protesting her innocence. Pursuant to the sentence, the body was conveyed to Edinburgh and handed over to Dr. Munro of the University for the purpose of dissection. It was said the Excise Officers at Pettycur were suspicious of the large box which contained the remains, and had it examined before it was allowed to cross the Forth.

[Several years later, an Irishman convicted of murder confessed that he was also responsible for this crime. He said that he was let into the house by the deceased after the servant girl had left. They had some drink together; a quarrel ensued and he struck Shuttleworth with a poker, but in order to divert suspicion he placed the weapon beside the sleeping woman. He then locked the door and made his escape by the chimney. Chimneys in those days were wide, and as the house was a one-storied building little difficulty would be experienced in getting away. There are cases on record of a housebreaker gaining admission by similar means. If the confession was true, it shows how a cunning scoundrel could by circumstances commit a crime and transmit the blame to another, thereby causing a misguided but innocent woman to suffer death. Of course, it cannot be affirmed with absolute certainty that the tramp's tragic utterance could be relied upon.

Mrs. Shuttleworth seems to have been a fatalist, as there was rather a curious coincidence with the date of the 20th September. On that day she was born in 1785. An accident occurred to her on the same date in 1796. She was married on the 20th September, 1806. Again, the warrant for her execution bore the same date in 1821. A curious little book, now very scarce, is in the writer's possession, and gives an account of the trial and execution. On the front page the lines of an old ballad appropriately appear: —

" Look thro' this prison's iron bars,
   Look thro' this dismal grate,
   And see how sin and drynkin brings
   So myserable a fate."]

November 16. George Thom, from Newmills, hanged at Aberdeen for poisoning his brother-in-law. Thom, attempted to poison the whole family with whom he had lately been connected by marriage. He committed the crimes in order to get money and property which he knew they possessed.

November 26 and 27. Before the High Court of Admiralty at Edinburgh, Peter Heaman, mate, and François Gautier, cook, of the schooner "Jane of Gibraltar," were charged with murder and piracy, committed on the schooner when on a voyage from Gibraltar to Brazil. The schooner was freighted with valuable merchandise, including specie to the amount of 38,180 Spanish dollars. A cabin boy, named Camelier, was the principal witness for the Crown. He deposed that upon the 18th June, Heaman beat the Captain to death after he had retired to rest, while Gautier shot the seaman at the helm with a musket. The bodies were then thrown overboard. Strachan and Smith (who were also witnesses) were confined in the hatchway, where the prisoners attempted to suffocate them. This was done by lighting a fire in the cabin and boring two holes in the bulkhead to let the smoke penetrate. The fire was kept burning continuously for two days, but at the end of that time the men were still alive. They were then taken out and made to swear on a Bible that they would not divulge anything that had happened. The course of the vessel having been altered after the murder of the Captain, Barra was reached about the middle of July, where a boat was procured to put ashore the dollars. The schooner was sunk and the money divided equally between the miscreants by the measure of a teapot. On reaching the shore the coins were buried among stones on the beach, where a dwelling tent was erected. This roused the attention of two Customs Officers, and the police were informed, who arrested the men.

No evidence was led for the defence. The Lord Advocate addressed the jury for the Crown, while Mr. Maitland (afterwards Lord Dundrennan) made a powerful speech for the defence. The Judge Admiral of Scotland, Sir John Connell, having concluded his summing-up at 6.30 a.m. on Tuesday, the 27th, the Court adjourned until 2.30 in the afternoon. The jury found both charges proved, and the men were sentenced to be detained in the Tolbooth of Edinburgh "until the second Wednesday of January next to come, being the ninth day of the said month of January, and upon that day, between the hours of nine o'clock morning and twelve noon, to be taken forth of the said Tolbooth to the Sands of Leith within floodmark, and there to be hanged on a gibbet." The Judge Admiral further ordained that the bodies should be delivered to Dr. Alexander Munro, Professor of Anatomy of Edinburgh University, for the purpose of dissection. His Lordship, in passing sentence, adverted strongly to the enormity of the crimes, and said: "If the law of this country permitted a punishment greater than death to be imposed on any case that punishment would be inflicted upon you, but although barbarians sometimes are to be found upon our shores, yet there is nothing barbarous in our laws." Holding out no hope of any respite, his Lordship said: "To the misguided and penitent offender the door of mercy is sometimes opened, but against the pirate and the murderer it will be for ever shut."

The sentences were duly carried into effect. The scaffold was erected at the foot of Constitution Street, Leith. Between eight and nine o'clock in the morning the procession left the "New Jail" (now the disused Calton Prison), and proceeded by Waterloo Place and Leith Walk. It was an imposing cavalcade. First came a detachment of the 3rd Dragoon Guards, a force of police, three carriages containing the Magistrates, and several ministers, a cart with the condemned man, while a strong body of police brought up the rear. All along the route there was a dense crowd. Heaman stood up bareheaded, and bowed respectfully as the procession moved forward, but his companion in crime was so much absorbed in thought that he paid no attention to the populace. The Admiral and Magistrates of Leith joined the procession at the foot of Leith Walk. Meanwhile the bell of South

Leith Parish Church began to toll. Heaman addressed the crowd for several minutes on the scaffold, and warned them to profit by his example. No fewer than 40,000 persons were present, but no untoward incident occurred.

[This was the last case of piracy in Scotland. The Admiralty Court was abolished in 1830, and its power vested with the Justiciary and Sheriff Courts.]

1822.

June 10 and 11. Before the High Court of Justiciary at Edinburgh, James Stuart, younger, of Dunearn, Fife, was charged with the murder of Sir Alexander Boswell of Auchinleck, Ayr, by engaging him in a duel at Balbarton, near Kirkcaldy, on the 26th March. Stuart was defended by Jeffrey, Moncreiff, and Cockburn, the greatest advocates then at the Scots Bar. On account of a scurrilous Whig song which had appeared in the "Sentinel," differences had arisen between the two parties, and it was therefore arranged to settle the dispute by means of a duel. A sequestered hollow on Balbarton was chosen. It was not far distant from Sir Alexander's residence at Balmuto. The distance measured was twelve paces from station to station, and the opponents took up their positions and received the pistols from their seconds. The word of command was given, and the pistol shots rang out, with the result that Sir Alexander lay prostrate on the ground while Stuart was unhurt. Sir Alexander was removed to Balmuto, where he died a few hours later. Stuart fled to France, but at length returned and stood his trial. In addition to the charge of murder it was also libelled that the prisoner conceived malice and illwill towards the deceased. Evidence was led and the Lord Advocate addressed the jury.

Mr. Jeffrey, in a powerful speech, said that it was not disputed that a duel had taken place, but that the provocation received was more than sufficient for fighting a duel. The law on the subject was carefully presented to the jury by the Lord Justice-Clerk, who said that no man, whatever his grievance, had the right to engage another in a duel. The trend of his Lordship's remarks was, however, not unfavourable to the accused. The jury, without retiring, after a few minutes' consultation, gave their verdict *vivâ voce* by their Chancellor, Sir John Hope of Craighall, Bart., finding the prisoner not guilty.

[The trial excited much interest among higher circles in Scotland. Stuart was accompanied in the dock by his relative, the Earl of Moray, Mr. Erskine of Cardross, and a number of other gentlemen. Several persons of distinction sat on the Bench with the judges, including Lord Belhaven and Stenton and the Honourable Henry Fox. A doggerel rhyme was current in Fife at that time:—

> '' For justice stood on Stuart's side,
>   Though he's awa' to France to bide;
>   And justice felled the Tory's pride,
>   That morning on Balbarton.'']

At Glasgow Circuit Court, James Campbell was sentenced to death for housebreaking. Lord Pitmilly, who passed sentence, had a curious request made by the prisoner: '' He hoped that his Lordship would not allow him to be brought into Court on his last day to attend Divine Service before a rabble. He, being a Protestant, desired the assistance of the clergy; he likewise hoped that though his Lordship and he had been enemies that day they would meet in Heaven.'' Lord Pitmilly with a paternal anxiety listened to the request, and assured the young man that over those matters he had no control, but he was certain the Magistrates would do everything in their power to accede to his request.

September 25. Edward Hand whipped through the streets of Glasgow for criminal assault at Greenock. The upper part of the body was completely uncovered. He received in all eighty strokes, but they were divided—twenty at the gaol, twenty at the lower end of Stockwell Street, twenty more at the end of Glassford Street, and the last twenty at the Cross. Some difference of opinion took place between the hangman and the Magistrates as to who was the proper person to undertake the menial duty of tying the culprit to the cart, and also who was to carry the spare '' cat o' nine tails '' in case the one in use became unfit for further service. The latter matter in dispute was, however, easily adjusted by putting the spare instrument of torture into a bag and slinging it from the end of the cart. A large crowd was present, but excellent order prevailed. Hand, pursuant to his sentence, was transported for life.

1823.

March 13, 14 and 15. Before the High Court of Justiciary at Edinburgh, Mary M'Kinnon was found guilty[a] of the murder by stabbing of a solicitor's clerk, in a brothel managed by her in the South Bridge, on the 8th February. She was hanged at the usual place of execution at the head of Libberton's Wynd, on the 16th April. It was estimated that no fewer than 20,000 persons were present. It is chronicled that no execution since that of Brodie in 1788 had excited so much sensation as this. The unfortunate woman was an officer's daughter, but had fallen into bad company. A ribald rhyme common in Edinburgh at that period commenced with the words:—

> " Mary M'Kinnon is my name,
> To misery I was born."

[She left all she possessed, about £4,000, to an English Jew with whom she had formed an attachment.]

October 29. Robert Scott (36), a gamekeeper, hanged at Fans Farm, near Earlston, Berwickshire. Scott had been convicted at Jedburgh Circuit Court, after a two days' trial before Lord Pitmilly, on the 17th September, of the murder of James Aitchison, a cooper in Greenlaw, and Robert Syme, a horse-dealer, also residing at Greenlaw. The affray, which was more or less a drunken quarrel, took place near Fans Farm, between Earlston and Greenlaw, when the men were returning form Earlston Fair on the 30th June.

The trial occasioned much public interest on the Borders, and Lord Minto and other noblemen occupied seats on the Bench. Lord Pitmilly passed sentence of death, to take effect as near the scene of the murder as convenient. Scott, who had been confined in Jedburgh Castle, had his irons struck off before nine o'clock in the morning on the fatal day of Wednesday, 29th October. He was handed to the Sheriff-Depute (the Sheriff Principal) and Magistrates of Jedburgh, all of whom were attired in deep mourning. Escorted by a company of the Roxburgh Yeomanry, the Sheriff and other officials proceeded to the County boundary, where Scott was handed over to the Sheriff Depute of Berwickshire. The boundary was the middle of the Leader Bridge, where a detachment of the Berwickshire Yeomanry were in waiting to act as escort. The procession then proceeded to the place of execution. Such a spectacle had not been witnessed in the Border district for years and attracted a great crowd. On the scaffold the unfortunate man was attended by the Rev. Mr. Gordon of Gordon. Scott had expressed a wish that the morning of his execution should be the most tempestuous which ever blew from the heavens so as to keep people away, but he was doomed to disappointment. The body was afterwards conveyed to Edinburgh to be dissected by Dr. Alexander Munro.

[Curious information regarding the various items incurred at the execution will be found in "An Old Berwickshire Town," by Robert Gibson. Among the entries are: Cutting Scott's hair, 2d. For shaving eleven times, 2d. each, 1/10. To a joiner for affixing a chair in a cart for conveying Scott to the place of execution, 3/6. For a cheese to men at the scaffold, 6d. For a lanthorn for escorting the corpse to Edinburgh, 3d. To a porter in Edinburgh conducting the cart to the place where the corpse was going, 1/-. To refreshment at Carfrae Mill for men and horse, 3/6. To victuals for eleven men watching the scaffold, £1 6/10. Mr. Gibson says that the men watching the scaffold amused themselves by playing cards, using the coffin made for Scott as a table. The total expenditure of carrying out the execution was £243 2/7.]

1825.

April 26. John Kean, a cotton spinner, was found guilty at Glasgow Circuit Court of attempting to murder a fellow-workman. Kean was sentenced to transportation for life, and also to be whipped on the 11th May, on a platform erected in front of the prison. The culprit received eighty strokes in all on the bare back with the "cat o' nine tails."

1826.

April 20. At Stirling Circuit Court, John M'Graddy was capitally convicted of housebreaking at the Manse of Muiravonside, on Sunday, 11th December. M'Graddy was hanged at Stirling on the 26th May.

[An unprecedented occurrence took place at this Circuit, as William Napier, trumpeter to the High Court, was killed by falling from his horse in the procession proceeding to the County Buildings in Broad Street.

Another unprecedented occurrence took place many years later at Aberdeen, when the minister who had hurried to the opening of the Circuit Court collapsed on the Bench while about to engage in prayer. Lord Deas, who was the judge, remarked after the body had been removed from his side that the circumstances were painful, and said, "Bring another minister."]

1827.

January 22. Before the High Court of Justiciary at Edinburgh, three men, William Thomson, John Thomson, and John Frame, all labourers, were sentenced to death for highway robbery. They assaulted and robbed a farmer at Cousland while riding home from Dalkeith Market, on the evening of the 30th November. The jury recommended the last two mentioned prisoners to the mercy of the Crown. The death sentence was fixed to be carried into effect at Dalkeith, "or at such place as the Sheriff shall fix," on Thursday, 1st March. The respite was granted to the two men whom the jury recommended to mercy, but William Thomson paid the full penalty. He was confined in the Calton Prison, Edinburgh, and removed to Dalkeith on the morning of the execution

A large crowd collected in Regent Road to witness the procession leave for Dalkeith. It consisted of four carriages and a number of officials and police on horseback. Sheriff Duff supervised the arrangements. Thomson's body, after execution, was delivered to his friends for burial.

April 14. Margaret Wishart was convicted at Perth Circuit

Court of poisoning her blind sister at Arbroath. On the scaffold she declared that she was not guilty, and said: "God will plead my cause." The act was done to win the affection of a young man who boarded with them, and who paid attention to her sister. She was hanged at Forfar on the 16th June.

September 26 and 27. At Aberdeen Circuit Court, Malcolm Gillespie, an exciseman well known for his prowess in tracking smugglers, was charged, along with his clerk, George Skene Edwards, with forging and uttering twenty-two different bills. They had adopted the names of farmers, and had traced their signatures on a window pane. Gillespie attributed his downfall to employing too many assistants—four or five being the usual number—and thus falling into debt. The jury retired at 1 a.m. to consider their verdict, and in the afternoon returned, finding proved eight of the charges of forgery and uttering against Gillespie, while Edwards was found guilty of forgery only. Mr. Neaves (afterwards Lord Neaves) stated objections to the latter verdict, and the case was certified for the opinion of the High Court.

The judges, Lords Pitmilly and Alloway, made special reference in passing sentence on Gillespie, to the altered circumstances in which he now stood. Frequently they had expressed approbation of his zeal and activity as an officer of the Revenue. "The recollection of those things has not been absent from our minds one single moment since the trial began, and I can scarcely make myself believe that such a reverse has taken place," continued Lord Pitmilly. Gillespie was sentenced to be hanged at Aberdeen on the 16th October. He wrote a life of himself and a dying declaration. The sentence was duly enforced at the usual place of execution in Aberdeen, "looking down Marischal Street."—a familiar saying of the populace when a person was hanged. Gillespie's body was handed over to his friends, and was interred in the churchyard of Skene.

[If the charge of forgery had not been proved there would still have been another charge against Gillespie for fire-raising. His cottage at Crombie was insured with two insurance companies to the extent of £8,300. The cottage was set on fire by two of his servants while Gillespie was on a visit to Edinburgh. Gunpowder and other combustibles had been placed on the premises. The two men pleaded guilty at the same Circuit to fire-raising, and the libel having been restricted from the capital offence, sentence of seven years' transportation was passed on each.

Edwards subsequently pleaded guilty to the charge of forgery before the Court at Edinburgh, and was sentenced on the 18th November to transportation for life. According to the existing custom a jury's verdict could be delivered verbally before the Court adjourned, but after an interval it required to be in writing and sealed in envelope. If the wax was black it was said to purport guilt (sentence of death). Scott, in "The Heart of Midlothian," chapter 25, makes reference to the breaking of the seal by the presiding judge, and the "unknown verdict," but, however, does not make any reference to the colour of the wax.]

November 6. Before the High Court at Edinburgh, a child, nine years old, named William Campbell, was sentenced to eighteen months' imprisonment in Bridewell for theft.

[This must surely be the most juvenile criminal that ever stood in the dock of the High Court.]

December 17. Before the High Court of Justiciary at Edinburgh, the Lord Justice-Clerk and Lords Gillies and Pitmilly on the Bench, Hugh M'Millan and Euphemia Lawson were charged with the murder of Archibald Campbell by throwing a quantity of sulphuric acid over his head and face, in consequence of which he died. They were also charged with the Statutory offence of attempt to murder. (This Statute, commonly known as Lord Ellenborough's Act, had recently been extended to Scotland). Campbell, who was their next door neighbour, had a quarrel with the prisoners, and they committed the acts out of revenge.

The Lord Advocate, after evidence had been led, departed from the charge of murder, but asked for a conviction for attempt to murder. After a short absence, the jury found the man not guilty, but convicted the woman, adding a recommendation to mercy. She was sentenced to be hanged at Edinburgh on the 23rd January.

[This was the first person capitally convicted in Scotland under the Ellenborough Act.]

1828.

December 24 and 25. Before the High Court of Justiciary
at Edinburgh, William Burke and Helen M'Dougall, his paramour,
were indicted on three charges of murder—(1) Mary Patterson,
a street walker; (2) " Daft Jamie," or James Wilson, an Edinburgh
" natural," and lastly, upon Margaret Docherty, an old woman.
Burke, who lived in Tanners' Close, West Port, Edinburgh, with
the woman, was joined in his ghoulish deeds of procuring bodies
for dissection by William Hare and his wife. The Crown had
decided with considerable reluctance that it would be dangerous
to put all four on trial, in case the evidence was not sufficient to
secure a conviction. Hare and his wife were thus admitted to
give King's evidence.

It has never been really decided whether Burke or Hare was
the greater villain. But the former originated the nefarious design
of decoying people to his house for the purpose of getting drink,
making them intoxicated, and then finally suffocating them when
they were powerless to offer much opposition. The "subjects,"
as they were termed, were sold to Dr. Knox, at Surgeons' Hall,
at £8 or £10 each, for dissecting purposes. Between December,
1827, and October, 1828, no fewer than sixteen persons were
disposed of in that manner by Burke and Hare. The crimes were
discovered through the death of the old woman Docherty. Mrs.
Gray, a friend of hers, knew that she was spending the night in
Burke's house. Along with her husband she went next morning,
and after various inquiries found the woman's dead body concealed
in straw in the house. Although told by Burke to say nothing
about it, she immediately informed the police, and the quartette
were arrested.

Speculation had been rife in many quarters of the city some
time previous as to what had become of the well-known character,
" Daft Jamie," who had suddenly disappeared from the streets.
Some students had, however, identified his body on the dissecting
table, but it was believed at first that he had not met his death
by foul play.

The trial commenced on Christmas Eve. (A curious date it
would be considered now to commence an important criminal trial,

but at that period this festival was not kept in Scotland). A bench of four judges were present, with the Lord Justice-Clerk (Boyle) in the chair. Sir William Rae, the Lord Advocate, with the assistance of Archibald Alison, Robert Dundas, and Alexander Wood, Advocates-Depute, conducted the prosecution. The prisoners, although destitute of funds, were according to custom given the services of the foremost pleaders of the day. Sir James W. Moncreiff, Bart., Dean of Faculty, defended Burke, while Mr. Cockburn (afterwards Lord Cockburn) defended the female prisoner. Among the witnesses for the Crown was William Hare. It has been said that "he entered the witness-box with a ghastly smile, and gave his infamous testimony with unblushing effrontery."* He was followed in the witness-box by his partner in life and in crime, whom the same eminent writer describes as "a truculent and forbidding hag, who bore in her arms a wretched infant then in the throes of whooping-cough." No evidence was led for the defence.

In his speech to the jury, the Lord Advocate said the chain of circumstantial evidence was complete against both prisoners. He described the acts as of "unexampled atrocity, unexampled in the history of civilised countries." The Dean of Faculty's address concluded at three o'clock in the morning, followed by Mr. Cockburn, who concluded two hours later. Even although the Court had sat almost continuously since the previous morning, the room was filled to its utmost capacity. The Lord Justice-Clerk concluded his charge at 8.30 a.m., which was on the whole against both prisoners. After an absence of fifty minutes, the jury found the charge against M'Dougall not proven, but the indictment proved against Burke. When the verdict was returned, Burke, with evident satisfaction, said: "Well, Nellie, you are out of the scrape."

In passing sentence, the Lord Justice-Clerk said: "Rest assured you have no chance of pardon. The only doubt I have in my mind in order to satisfy the violated laws of your country and the voice of the public indignation is whether your body should not be exhibited in chains to bleach in the winds, to deter others from the commission of such offences, but taking into consideration

---

*Notable British Trial Series: "Burke and Hare," by William Roughead.

the public eye would be offended by such a dismal spectacle, I am willing to accede to a more lenient execution of your sentence, that your body should be publicly dissected." Burke was hanged on the 28th January, 1829. An immense crowd hooted him on the scaffold, while above the din could be heard cries, "Where is Hare?"—the popular feeling being that he had been too generously treated by the Crown.

Sir Walter Scott and Charles Kilpatrick Sharpe witnessed the execution from the window of 423 High Street.* "Christopher North" (Professor Wilson), who was present at the trial, described Hare as "the most brutal man that was ever subjected to my sight." Burke, the same writer says, "was a neat little man about five feet five." The description of the woman in the dock was not flattering: "A poor, miserable, boney, skinny, scranky, wizend jade." Burke's body was open to view at Surgeons' Hall, when 24,000 persons, including some women, passed through the room.

[This arch-villain has enriched the English language with the verb "to burke." The trial created a great sensation. Douce citizens looked askance at the revelations. Dr. Knox was mobbed, and had to leave Edinburgh. Considerable difficulty was experienced in getting Hare out of the city, but ultimately the authorities succeeded by means of a disguise. He proceeded to London, and eked out an existence as a beggar in Oxford Street. A ribald rhyme tersely summed up the principal actors in this terrible case:—

> " Up the close and down the stair,
> But and ben with Burke and Hare.
> Burke's the butcher, Hare's the thief,
> Knox the boy who buys the beef."

The Anatomy or Warburton's Act of 1832 put an end to the disgusting trade of dealing in dead bodies.]

1829.

August 19. John Stuart and his wife, Catherine Wright or Stuart, were hanged at Edinburgh for poisoning a passenger,

*" The Royal Mile," by R. T. Skinner.

named John Lamond, on the "Toward Castle," between Tarbert and Glasgow. According to the evidence, the prisoners repeatedly supplied drink to Lamond and his friends while on the boat. They were seen to put something into a mug of porter, which was forced upon Lamond while insensible. He was subsequently robbed of a purse and a sum of money. On the arrival of the boat at Glasgow, Lamond was found to be in a state of stupor, and died next day. His friends, although seriously ill, gradually recovered. Stuart and his wife disappeared whenever the boat was berthed at the Broomielaw, and were afterwards arrested. A purse, which was identified as having belonged to Lamond, was found in Stuart's possession.

1830.

March 17. Robert Edmund hanged at Edinburgh for the murder of Mrs. Franks and her daughter, near Haddington. Edmund was a brother-in-law of the deceased, and committed the act against Mrs. Franks out of revenge. The prisoner did not cherish any ill-will against his niece, but thought she would betray him.

September 8. At Perth Circuit Court, John Henderson, a loom worker, was charged with the murder of his employer, named Millie, at Whinny Park, Monimail, Fife. Henderson beat the deceased to death in the loom shop, and attempted to bury the body there, but the earth was too shallow. He then dragged the body to the garden, about sixty yards distant, and there buried it. The murder was committed for the purpose of robbery, as Henderson presented a deposit receipt for £40 at the bank with a forged signature which belonged to Millie. Henderson also removed several articles from the house, and sold them as belonging to himself. He disappeared, but was arrested several weeks later at Dunfermline. In addition to the murder charge, two others, theft and forgery, were libelled against him. After an absence of four minutes, the jury found all the charges proved. Lord Meadowbank passed sentence of death, to be carried out at Cupar, on the 30th September. Henderson confessed his guilt, and duly paid the penalty. No fewer than 20,000 persons were present at the final scene.

D

October 8. Mrs. Humphrys hanged at Aberdeen for the murder of her husband. Both the deceased and the prisoner were much addicted to drink. The woman, who kept a public-house in Aberdeen, had several times threatened him with violence, with the result that the husband had prophesied "that she would yet hang with her face towards Marischal Street." During sleep she administered to her husband a teaspoonful of oil of vitriol, which resulted in the man dying in great agony. The woman confessed her guilt. Forty-five years had passed since a woman had been hanged at Aberdeen.

[The saying of "facing Marischal Street" was at one time a common expression among the criminal classes of Aberdeen. It was often said in sheer bravado that one would do something even although "he should face Marischal Street," or in other words, be hanged. This is synonymous with the Glasgow term, "that he would face the Monument for it."]

1831.

March 14. Before the High Court of Justiciary at Edinburgh, James M'Gowan was sentenced to seven years' transportation, and to be whipped through the town of Haddington, for assault.

[This was the last instance of a corporal pain being pronounced by the High Court.]

July 13 and 14. Before the High Court of Justiciary at Edinburgh, George Gilchrist, an innkeeper at Hillend, near Bathgate, was sentenced to death for robbing the "Prince Regent" coach of £5,700 in notes, belonging to the Commercial Banking Company, on the 24th March. A charge against two other men was found not proven. Gilchrist was part owner of the coaches running between Glasgow and Edinburgh by Airdrie. When his share in the business was realised, 50 horses were sold for £1,400. A box containing the notes had been abstracted from the boot of the coach by cutting a hole from the inside. Gilchrist was hanged at Edinburgh on 3rd August. He collapsed on the scaffold and had to be supported by two men.

September 26. At Inverness Circuit Court, Hector M'Leod was convicted of the murder of Murdoch Grant, a pedlar, whom he had also robbed at Assynt in March, 1830. Grant had disappeared, but after four weeks his body was found floating in a mountain lake. From marks on the body, and also the fact that the pockets were turned out, it was evident the deceased had met his death by foul play. M'Leod (who like his great rival in crime, Eugene Aram, had been a schoolmaster), was foremost in assisting the Sheriff to clear up the mystery. After some time passed it was brought to the Sheriff's notice that M'Leod had changed a £10 note at a Post Office. When interrogated as to where the note came from, his reply was unsatisfactory.

Kenneth Fraser, a tailor, afterwards known as "The Dreamer," came forward with a remarkable story. He said the murder had been revealed to him in a dream, and he informed the authorities where the pedlar's pack was to be found, in a cairn of stones. On investigation being made, certain articles belonging to Grant were found at the cairn, and M'Leod was arrested.

The trial had been fixed for the Autumn Circuit in 1830, but as sufficient jurymen were not present it was adjourned until the next sitting of the Court at Inverness, in April, 1831. (In those days there were no special sittings of the Court as there are now). Once again, however, the trial was postponed, on account of the absence of a material witness, and in order that additional evidence could be obtained. For a whole year M'Leod was confined in the Old Jail at Inverness; the more recent and commanding building known as "The Castle" (which in turn has given way to the modern prison at Porterfield) was then not built.

The trial, as it has been said, ultimately took place on the 26th September. The judges were Lords Moncreiff and Medwyn. All day and throughout the night the proceedings lasted. "The grey light of morning was beginning to be visible through the Courtroom windows" when Lord Moncreiff began his charge to the jury. After an absence of 15 minutes the jury found both charges proved. (There was a charge of theft libelled). M'Leod, who seemed surprised at the verdict, exclaimed: "The Lord Almighty knows that I am innocent. I did not think that anyone in this County would be condemned on mere opinion." Sentence of death was passed, to be carried out on the 24th October. Later M'Leod confessed his guilt.

The scaffold had been erected at "The Longman," to the east of the town. The procession was grim and weird—perhaps indeed unprecedented at any similar proceedings. M'Leod was arrayed in a long black robe, with a white cap on his head, while a rope was round his neck, the end of which was held by the hangman. Carrying a Bible in his hands, M'Leod sang parts of the Psalms, which was taken up by the dense crowd as the procession passed along. On his arrival at the scaffold, a religious service was held, and the condemned man addressed the multitude in Gaelic. On his giving the usual signal by dropping a handkerchief, the bolt was drawn. Three-quarters of an hour later the body was placed in a coffin for removal to Edinburgh, for the purpose of dissection.

[This remarkable case is mentioned in Chambers's "Book of Days," Vol. I., page 394., and also in "Fraser's Magazine," for December, 1856.]

October 20. William Heath hanged at Glasgow for robbing Watson's Bank, Virginia Street, of £6,000. Heath was convicted at the Autumn Circuit. A woman, named Elizabeth Crowder, was also charged with the robbery, but the indictment was found not proven. On the day after the robbery, Monday, Heath left Glasgow under an assumed name for London, and at Dover was found exchanging Scotch bank notes for French gold. The robbery, which had been accomplished by false keys, was deliberately planned. Some weeks previous to the robbery, Heath had paid several visits to an ironmonger in Glasgow to get suitable blank keys made.

1832

January 19. Samuel Waugh hanged at Ayr, for the murder of a special constable named Ross, during the riots at Girvan, on the 12th July, 1831. The village people attempted to prevent an Orange demonstration from Maybole entering the town. Desperate encounters took place, guns and swords being freely used. Waugh, an Orangeman and one of the leaders of the procession, took deliberate aim with a gun at Ross, who fell dead. Waugh fled but was soon captured.

The trial took place before the High Court of Justiciary at Edinburgh in December. The prisoner was removed to Ayr under a strong force of the Ayrshire Yeomanry, who also formed a guard around the scaffold. Upwards of 5,000 persons were present when the bolt was drawn.

[A little north of Girvan Station, on the road to Maybole, there is a stone which bears the following inscription: "On this spot, Alexander Ross, special constable, was shot dead whilst in the execution of his duty. 12th July, 1831."]

January 21. John Howison, a pedlar, was hanged at Edinburgh, for the murder of a widow named Geddes, at Cramond. He made a startling declaration on the night before his execution, when he confessed to having been guilty of six murders, four of his victims being children in Edinburgh. The crimes, he said, were committed while he was under the influence of drink. Howison also confessed to having stolen, during his travels, four gold and a number of silver watches, but he denied having murdered the woman. It is stated that the confessions were hardly credible, but all the same he spoke with the utmost composure. No relatives nor friends visited Howison during his confinement.

October 31. John Chisholm (76), hanged at Perth for wife murder. Chisholm, who had carried on a merchant's business in South Street, Perth, for about forty years, was a devout church attender and a member of the special constables. He had married twice. His first wife, with whom he did not live on friendly terms, prophesied that " one day he would be hanged, although she would not live to see it." The prisoner protested his innocence to the last. On the scaffold he conducted himself with considerable composure. A portion of a Psalm was sung, in which he joined audibly. After an impressive prayer from the Chaplain, Chisholm asked that the 5th Hymn should be sung. After a few minutes in prayer, he dropped the handkerchief and was launched into eternity. The multitude assembled "was very great." Such a spectacle had not taken place in the city since the execution of Wyllie and Clark, on the same day seventeen years previous. The ground was kept by a company of the 79th Highlanders. The body was buried within the prison wall, next to South Street.

[All the names of the murderers who had suffered the full penalty could be seen inscribed on the prison wall until a few years ago, when the wall was removed to widen the street. There were also a skull and cross bones, with the words, Genesis, chap. 9, verse 6: "Whoso sheddeth man's blood, by man shall his blood be shed."]

1834.

January 20. Hugh Kennedy (27) was hanged at Glasgow, for throwing vitriol in the face of the hotel "boots" at the Buck's Head Inn. Kennedy had been assistant to the "boots," and had quarrelled over his wages. He was convicted at the Circuit in December.

[This was the last occasion where a capital conviction under the Ellenborough Act for attempt to murder was carried out. Martin Doyle, at Chester, on the 26th August, 1861, was the last person hanged in England under this Act.]

April 1. Mannes Swiney, an Irish reaper, who had been convicted at Edinburgh, was hanged at Greenlaw, for assaulting and robbing a labourer between Lauder and Stow, on the 24th September. The scaffold was erected in front of the County Hall. Swiney was attended in his last days by a Roman Catholic Priest, who stated to the crowd that the condemned man desired him to say that he denied all participation in the robbery. The jury had coupled the verdict with a recommendation to mercy, but Lord Melbourne declined to interfere.

May 31. William Noble (20), hanged at Elgin, for the murder of William Ritchie, on the public road near Lhanbryde, in December. Noble had been in the army, but had deserted. He met Ritchie, and during a quarrel inflicted fatal injuries with a stick. Noble was convicted at Inverness Circuit Court on the 5th May. He acknowledged the justice of his sentence in his dying declaration, in the course of which he said that "the judge, jury, witnesses and others who were the means, under the direction of Almighty God, who never slumbers or sleeps, of bringing home the guilty actions to me, all acted honestly and justly in convicting me of the offence."

[Curiously, Lhanbryde figured prominently in another murder trial where an Army deserter also paid the full penalty. (See 1908).]

October 23. John Boyd, a hat merchant, hanged at Greenock for wife murder. Boyd had been convicted at Glasgow Circuit Court in September, but a respite of fourteen days was granted from the original date of the warrant, 9th October. During the forenoon the shops in the vicinity of the scaffold were closed. A numerous body of special constables were on duty, but we read, "the most perfect order prevailed throughout the whole proceedings."

1835.

September 18. At Inverness Circuit Court, John Adam (31), an ex-soldier, was convicted before Lord Moncreiff of wife murder. The body of the deceased, whose maiden name was Janet Brechin, was discovered in a ruined hut, partially buried, at Milbuie, in the Black Isle of Ross-shire. Death had evidently been caused by foul play. Suspicion rested upon a man known as John Anderson, who lived with a woman as his wife at Dingwall, and he was arrested. Adam had for some time acted in a dual capacity, as witnesses, including the Parish Minister of Laurencekirk (who married them), testified that Adam, known to them as Anderson, was really the husband of Janet Brechin. After the marriage the couple had proceeded to Inverness. The woman had given up her shop and had drawn her savings at the bank, amounting to £113. After staying in Inverness for a few days, Adam, on the pretext that he had taken a house near Tarradale, induced his wife to accompany him. She was never seen alive again. A sum of £75 was found under Adam's pillow when he was arrested, but he said that it belonged to an aunt who had just died. His statement, however, turned out to be a mere fabrication of falsehoods.

During his incarceration after sentence, Adam declined to make a confession. The condemned man, dressed in a black camlet cloak, was drawn to the place of execution, "The Longman," and hanged there on the 10th October. It had been originally decided that Adam was to walk in the procession like the last person executed (see M'Leod in 1831), but in case he should escape in the crowd along the route he was placed in a cart. After the execution a fellow-prisoner said that Adam acknowledged to him the justice of his sentence, and he had his authority to make that known after his death. Adam was interred beneath a flag-stone in the Old Jail, and was buried in a standing position.

1837.

March 18. Before the High Court of Justiciary at Edinburgh, Alexander Miller was convicted of murder and theft near Denny-loanhead. He was hanged at Stirling on the 8th April. As Miller was a young and desperate character, it was thought advisable to place a rope round his waist, which was held from a window in the Jail, in case he should leap from the scaffold and make a scene. Even with this device he was not prepared to let the occasion pass without being troublesome, for he managed to take off a shoe and throw it among the crowd. This was followed by a handkerchief, which he was supposed to drop at his feet as a signal to the hang-man that he was ready. The hangman wore a black wig, and was disguised.

October 18. William Pirrie, who had been convicted of wife murder at the Glasgow Circuit in September, was hanged in front of the County Buildings, Paisley. Pirrie, in a fit of jealousy, on returning home from his work locked the children out of the house and then with a three-edged file inflicted fatal injuries upon his wife. The prisoner admitted the crime, which he said was·done while he was in a state of temporary frenzy. The Edinburgh hangman officiated, and earned the following eulogium from the newspapers: "The feelings of the crowd and the prisoner were saved from all unnecessary torture."

1838.

April 14. At Inverness Circuit Court, Malcolm M'Lean, a fisherman from Clete, on the island of Bayle, Lewis, was sentenced to death for wife murder. The prisoner admitted his guilt, but on the advice of his counsel pleaded not guilty. Evidence was then led. Being a religious fanatic was pleaded by the defence. The execution was fixed to take place at Inverness on the 11th May, but the sentence was commuted.

[Lord Cockburn, who was the presiding judge, alludes to this case at some length in his " Circuit Journeys."]

May 21. Mrs. Jaffray hanged at Glasgow, for poisoning Ann Carole and Hugh Munro at Carluke, in October. They were lodgers in her house, and were poisoned with arsenic, which was procured for the purpose of killing rats. Mrs. Jaffray scornfully refused to make any confession of the crimes. She appeared on the scaffold in all the glory of a Rob Roy tartan shawl.

[After the execution the Rob Roy tartan went into great disfavour, and no woman was seen wearing it again for many years.]

1839.

March 25. Before the High Court of Justiciary at Edinburgh, Arthur Wood and Henrietta Young or Wood were charged with the murder of John Drew Wood, a pedlar, the son of the prisoner by a former marriage. The tragedy was committed in Thorter Row, Dundee, where the deceased suffered terrible injuries. His head was dashed against a wall; afterwards he was strangled with a rope. The jury found the charge proved against Wood, but by a majority not proven regarding his wife. Wood was sentenced to be hanged at Dundee on the 18th April, but a week's respite was granted before he paid the penalty.

1840.

April 16. James Wemyss, an umbrella maker, hanged at Edinburgh for wife murder.

[A respite had been granted for ten days, and some difference of opinion existed among the Magistrates as to when the respite expired. Their Lordships, who had heard the case, subsequently met in private and decided the point. The execution was not carried through with dispatch, as for some reason unknown the hangman withdrew the wrong bolt. In consequence, the drop did not fall, while hisses and groans rent the air from the crowd. It was not until an official in attendance ran upstairs to the scaffold and released the proper bolt that the man's sufferings were at an end.]

1841.

April 23. At Glasgow Circuit Court, before Lord Moncreiff, three Irish labourers, Dennis Doolan, Patrick Reeding, and James

Hickie, employed on the Edinburgh and Glasgow Railway at Bishopbriggs, were sentenced to death for the murder of a ganger, named John Green, at Crosshill, on the 17th December. National feeling was assigned as the cause of the murder. The Solicitor-General who prosecuted said that after the evidence he would not detain the jury by a word of remark. Mr. Patrick Robertson, for the prisoners, said he did not see that he could, with advantage to the men, analyse the evidence, and would therefore leave the case to the jury, hoping if there was a doubt they would give them the benefit. The jury found Doolan and Reeding guilty as libelled, and by a majority found James Hickie guilty, not as actor but art and part, unanimously recommending him to mercy. Lord Moncreiff passed sentence of death on each. The execution was fixed to be carried out on the 14th May, "at or near Crosshill, in the Parish of Cadder," where the tragedy had taken place. The Home Secretary, Lord Normanby, granted a respite to Hickie, who is described as "one of the most perfectly ignorant men in the world, as he can neither read nor write."

[No mention is made in the Press why the Solicitor-General conducted the prosecution in person, which is, of course, quite unusual at Circuit, the duties being left exclusively to the Advocates-Depute.]

Dennis Doolan and Patrick Reeding were duly hanged. As a report was current that an attempt at rescue would be made by their comrades, three pieces of artillery and a strong force of military held the precincts of the scaffold. The procession left the Jail at the Green and proceeded by the Saltmarket and the Kirkintilloch Road to Crosshill. A formidable force of military and police led the way. The condemned men were seated in a cart, attended by Roman Catholic priests. The Sheriffs and Magistrates were in carriages, while the hangman was seated in a cab. A party of the 1st Royal Dragoons and two companies of the 58th Foot acted as escort on each side.

It was a wonderful display of pomp and panoply, which was supposed to act as a deterrent against the commission of such crimes in future. At certain points it was with the greatest difficulty that a passage could be forced, as thousands of spectators lined the streets. Everything passed off satisfactorily, and the bodies, after hanging the usual time, were put into coffins, and the procession returned to town in the same order as before. The bodies were buried within the prison.

A newspaper report says: "Thousands of men, and women too, turned out on this occasion without compunction, delicacy, or shame. None who saw the great multitude could doubt the popularity of the show. A royal triumph could not have excited a stronger desire on the part of the public to witness it. Windows were taken and paid for, and the housetops were crowded. It was estimated that at least 75,000 persons lined the route and surrounded the scaffold."

Alexander Smith, in his "Dreamthorp," gives a most vivid description of the scene.

1842.

January 6. James Bowers and others, medical students—duellists and seconds—were each sentenced to two months imprisonment, and also to find £50 security for their good behaviour, by the High Court of Justiciary at Edinburgh, for engaging in a duel. One of the parties was injured in the thigh.

[They were charged under the Breach of the Peace Act. This was the last case in Scotland regarding duels. It has been said that the late distinguished judge, Lord Shand, was one of the principals in the last duel which took place in this country. It was under the shadow of Arthurs Seat, in the "fifties," when Mr. Shand, as he was then, met his fellow-duellist. Fortunately there were no fatal consequences, as unknown to them their seconds had loaded the pistols with powder only. The last fatal duel in England was fought at Portsmouth, between Lieutenants Hawkey and Seton, the latter being killed, on 20th May, 1845.]

April. It is reported in the newspapers that at the ensuing Circuit Court at Perth there were no fewer than 600 witnesses cited for the various trials. The cases were 85 in number, 35 of which were from Dundee. As the City Police had been much reduced in numbers, the Lord Provost and Magistrates applied for a guard of military. Accordingly, a company of the 93rd Highlanders arrived in Perth from Dundee. It is also stated that with one exception, at Glasgow, where the number exceeded the foregoing by one, this is the largest number of cases which have ever been indicted at any Circuit in Scotland.

April 16 and 17. At Aberdeen Circuit Court, a Russian Jew, named Rosenberg, and his wife, at one time an actress, were found guilty of fire-raising in their house in Aberdeen. Sentence was postponed.

[This was a remarkable trial. The case commenced on Saturday, the 16th, but did not conclude until the following morning, Sunday, at 12.30 a.m. As the business of the Inverness Circuit opened on Monday, the Junior Judge, Lord Cockburn, and the Circuit Clerk, had to leave, and Lord Moncreiff, who by the way was a strict Sabbatarian, concluded the sitting himself. Mr. John Dunn, Advocate in Aberdeen, had been appointed Interim Clerk, and the oath was administered to him. On account of the jury's recommendation of leniency, and also to the "unusual circumstances in which the trial had concluded," Lord Moncreiff did not pass sentence, but certified the case to the High Court of Justiciary at Edinburgh for opinion of a bench of judges. This is the only instance of a trial in Scotland extending into Sunday morning.]

1843.

May 18. Charles Mackay hanged at Glasgow for wife murder. They had been drinking together and both had fallen asleep. On awakening, Mackay ordered her to make some breakfast. She was quite unable to do so, and being in an irritable mood, Mackay stabbed her. Dressed in a suit of black, with a white necktie, and carrying a letter in his hand, Mackay mounted the scaffold. The letter was addressed to the Lord Provost, Sir James Campbell, and was in lieu of making a speech on the scaffold, as was customary. In a long statement he warned married couples to avoid drink, and said the crime was not premeditated.

September 13. At Stirling Circuit Court, Allen Mair, lately residing at Candie End, Muiravonside, was found guilty of wife murder. Both were about eighty years of age. Mair had led a somewhat chequered career. In his early days he had settled in the States, but subsequently returned home. He then rented a small farm near Stirling, but fell into debt by litigation. Latterly he removed to a small cottage at Candie End. For years he had ill-treated his wife, and finally murdered her. When Lord Moncreiff asked him if he had anything to say before sentence was passed, Mair denied that he had committed murder.

On the day of the execution, the 4th October, the condemned man refused to walk to the scaffold, and had to be carried in an armchair and placed under the drop. An extraordinary scene then ensued, perhaps unprecedented. Mair, in a loud voice, began to curse everyone, including the minister, Sheriff, Fiscal, and witnesses. In the midst of a terrible outburst, he said: " The meenister o' the paarish invented lees against me. Folks, yin an' a', mind I'm nae murderer. I ne'er committed murder, and I say it as a dyin' man who is about to pass into the presence of his Goad. I was condemned by the lees o' the meenister, by the injustice of the Sheriff and Fiscal, and perjury of the witnesses. I trust for their conduct that a' thae parties shall be overta'en by the vengeance of Goad, and sent into everlasting damnation. I curse them wi' the curses in the Hunner and Ninth Psalm— ' Set thou a wicked man o'er them '—an' haud on thee, hangman, till I'm dune—' An' let Satan stand at their richt haun. Let their days be few, let their children be faitherless, let their weans be continually vagabonds '; and I curse them a'." The hangman at length put an end to the old man's spiteful opprobriums by withdrawing the bolt. But Mair was not done yet. As his hands had not been properly secured, he made a clutch at the rope, and at first it appeared that he would be able to free himself. The hangman, however, pulled away his hands, and within a minute or so death had fulfilled the law.

1844.

January 12 and 13. Before the High Court of Justiciary at Edinburgh, the Lord Justice-Clerk (Hope) and Lords Moncreiff and Wood on the Bench, Christina Gilmour was charged with the murder of her husband, a farmer, at Inchinnan, Renfrew. The body had been exhumed, and in consequence of the *post mortem* a warrant was issued for her apprehension. It was ascertained that she was on her way to America, travelling under the name of Mrs. Spiers. Superintendent Mackay, of the Renfrew Police, however, arrived in New York before her, and effected her arrest. She was the first person to be extradited under Lord Ashburton's Treaty of 1842.

The evidence adduced by the Crown showed that the prisoner, a daughter of Mr. Cochrane, of the Grange, Dunlop, was in love with a neighbouring farmer, John Anderson, Broadley. Her affection was reciprocated by him. They had been friendly all their lives, having been brought up as boy and girl together. Her father, however, did not favour this union, and at his instigation she married John Gilmour, Townhead, Inchinnan. The marriage was a failure, and within five months of the ceremony the husband was dead. He was buried in Dunlop Churchyard, but, as it has been said, the body was exhumed. Mr. Cochrane had meantime sent his daughter to America. No information where she had gone was vouchsafed by the relatives, and the authorities had much difficulty in locating her.

Mary Paterson, a servant girl, who had been employed by the accused, stated that she had bought arsenic for her mistress in Paisley, on the pretext it was for rats. The prisoner, in her declaration, admitted that she had bought poison in Renfrew under an assumed name, but it was for putting an end to herself, as her life was so unhappy. Mr. Maitland (afterwards Lord Dundrennan) made a powerful appeal on her behalf, and asked for a verdict of not proven. The summing-up of the Lord Justice Clerk was not unfavourable to the accused. After an absence of an hour the jury found the charge not proven. The verdict was received in Court with great applause. "Kirsty" Cochrane, as she was familiarly termed in her own district, thus left the dock a free woman.

[Mrs. Gilmour remained unmarried, and died at Stewarton, Ayrshire, in 1906, at the great age of 87. She was honoured and respected by all who knew her.

It may be added that thirteen years later a similar verdict, before the same judge, was returned in the Madeleine Smith case.]

April 3. James Bryce hanged at Edinburgh, for the murder of his brother-in-law, near West Calder, on the 27th December.

Bryce made a detailed confession, and gave a most minute description of the tragedy. (See 1864).

1848.

April 27. At Perth Circuit Court, James Robertson was convicted of the murder of his illegitimate child. He was hanged at Forfar on the 19th May.

[A stone on the north wall of the prison yard, with " J. R., 19th May, 1848," denotes his burying place.]

October 4 and 5. At Ayr Circuit Court, James M'Whellan was convicted of the murder of a young lad, named James Young, a farm servant, at Fortyacres, Kilmarnock. He was hanged at Ayr on the 26th October.

[An old couplet commemorates the event:—

" 'Twas on Kilmarnock Fast and Glasgow Fair,
Was the day M'Whellan was hanged at Ayr."]

1849.

April 24. At Aberdeen Circuit Court, James Burnett, a farm servant, was convicted of wife murder by administering arsenic. Mrs. Burnett, who was an invalid, died suddenly. A fortnight later, Burnett, who some time previous to his wife's death had been paying attention to a servant girl, put in " the cries " of marriage between them. They were duly proclaimed in Fyvie Church. Suspicion, however, was aroused, and the body was exhumed, when 23 grains of arsenic was found in the stomach. Burnett was hanged at Aberdeen on the 22nd May.

April 27. At Perth Circuit Court, John Kellocher, a young Irish labourer, was convicted of the murder of a woman, at Butter-gask, some two miles south of Blackford, in November. Kellocher, while working on the Scottish Central Railway four years previous, had lodged with the deceased, Jenny Anderson. She kept a refreshment shop, and resided there with her son, who was the village blacksmith. Kellocher being again in the neighbourhood, resolved to give her a call. Unfortunately it was Communion Sabbath day, and all were at Church except the woman. He was

hospitably received, and as he could see no one about the tempta-
tion that there was money in the house proved too much for him.
Seizing a hatchet, he struck the woman several blows, and then
ransacked the house for money.

Large crowds thronged to the Fair City to witness the
execution. The scaffold was erected at the south wall of the
prison. The total expense of the execution was £117 7/6.

October 4. At Jedburgh Circuit Court, Thomas Wilson and
John Brady, navvies, were sentenced to death for the murder of
a shepherd, named William Lauder, during a riot at St. Boswell's
Fair Day, at Kelso, in July. Four hundred navvies attempted
to rescue a prisoner from the custody of the police, and Lauder
gallantly went to their assistance. In the disturbance he was
beaten to death. Order was restored only on the arrival of the
2nd Dragoons from Piershill, when the prisoners were arrested.
Wilson was hanged in front of the Castle at Jedburgh, on the
25th October, but Brady's sentence was commuted to transportation for life.

[Sir Walter Scott had intimate association with the Jedburgh
Circuit. It was there, on the first occasion after his becoming
an advocate, that he defended a prisoner in a criminal case. This
was a well-known poacher, who was acquitted. He thanked his
counsel quite audibly in Court, and asked if Scott would like
" a maukin " in the morning as an extra fee. On another occasion
Scott was defending a housebreaker. When he asked his client
what was the best preventive against a nocturnal visitor, the man
replied: "A barking dog and rusty lock." The advice Scott
turned into rhyme:—

> " A yelping terrier, rusty key,
> Was Walter Scott's best Jeddart fee."

For twenty years, without hardly a break, spring and autumn,
he attended the Circuit, first as counsel, and latterly as Sheriff.

The holding of a Court in a Circuit Town is of very ancient
origin. We read in the Bible: "Samuel went from year to year
in circuit to Bethel, Gilgal, and Mispeh," three places which
were once likened to the three towns making up the South Circuit,

of which Jedburgh is one, Dumfries and Ayr the others. The well-known phrase, "Jeddart Justice," is proverbial. It was generally supposed that this term was used as a reproach against justice meted out to offenders at Jedburgh, but this does not seem to be consistent with facts. The origin of the phrase as given by Scott in his "Minstrelsy" is that, about the beginning of the century, lawlessness prevailed to such an extent that severe measures had to be adopted. Circuit Courts are from time to time yet held at Jedburgh, and the time-honoured procession still takes place, as in Scott's time, from the ancient hostelry, "The Spread Eagle," to the County Buildings.]

1850.

January 31. Mrs. Hamilton, or Mary Lennox, hanged at Glasgow, for poisoning her sister-in-law, at Strathaven. She collapsed in a faint and had to be supported on each side before the bolt was drawn. Murdoch, the hangman, was then over eighty years of age, and ascended the scaffold with the aid of a stick.

April 19. At Jedburgh Circuit Court, before Lords Mackenzie and Ivory, James Deary and Daniel O'Rouskie, railway navvies, were charged with the murder, by stabbing, of William Fairbairn, a horse-dealer, at Kelso, on the 29th December. Deary was found guilty with a strong recommendation to mercy, while the charge against the other man was found not proven. Lord Mackenzie passed sentence of death, to be carried out in front of the Castle, Jedburgh, on the 10th May, but the penalty was commuted.

[This was the last capital sentence pronounced at Jedburgh.]

August 16. William Bennison hanged at Edinburgh, for wife murder and bigamy. He resided at Stead's Place, Leith Walk. A deeply religious man, he was sometimes known as "Holy Willie Bennison." His wife died on the 15th April, and was buried in Rosebank Cemetery.* The finger of suspicion pointed to her husband. Probably this would not have happened and the death of Mrs. Bennison would have been unavenged, but for a curious circumstance. The dog of a blind man who lived below the

---

* See Appendix, page 151.

E

prisoner's house died after having partaken of some porridge that the deceased had taken when she became ill. It was discovered that Bennison had bought arsenic from a chemist in the Kirkgate, Leith, and had asked him as a favour not to disclose the purchase. Bennison had contracted a marriage, twelve months previous, with an Irish girl at Portadown, but had deserted her.

Large crowds assembled to witness Bennison go to his doom. Many well-known ladies had seats at the Advocates' Library to watch the grim proceedings. Murdoch, of Glasgow, was the hangman. A street ballad of that period described the final scene : —

> " Great was the throng to see him hung
>   For crimes that were so vile.
> To Edinburgh upon that day
>   They tramped for many a mile.
> They led him out all clad in black—
>   Black coat and vest so white—
> A mocking smile was on his lips,
>   He wore a nosegay bright."

1851.

October 2. At Glasgow Circuit Court, before Lord Colonsay, Archibald Hare (27) was found guilty of fatally stabbing a man at Blantyre. The prisoner was described in the newspapers as "of repulsive and dogged aspect." He was hanged on the 24th October. The execution was a terrible spectacle, as after the bolt was drawn the unfortunate man dropped two feet and then spun round like a top, all the while making vain efforts by his pinioned hands to catch the rope. Murdoch, the old hangman, however, swung himself from the legs of the man, and held on until death happily supervened.

[Hare was believed to be a nephew of William Hare, of the Burke and Hare atrocities.]

1852.

April 28. At Perth Circuit Court, before Lord Cockburn, Charles Fancoat was convicted of stabbing fatally a fellow-labourer, Michael Harrigan, in the High Street, Dunfermline, on the 14th February. He was sentenced to be hanged at Dunfermline on the 25th May. The Rev. Dr. M'Michael, and other influential citizens of the burgh, made herculean efforts to secure a commutation of the sentence, and were successful. Mr. Logan, for the defence, pleaded for a verdict of culpable homicide. Lord Cockburn described the tragedy as "the united influences of intoxication and passion."

[This was the last person under sentence of death at Dunfermline.]

June 14. Before the High Court of Justiciary at Edinburgh, the Lord Justice-General and Lords Cockburn and Cowan on the Bench, Michael and Peter Scanlan, two brothers, natives of County Mayo, were charged with murder and stouthrief (robbery with violence), committed at Hilton of Forthar, Fife. The men were employed at the adjacent lime works, and lodged next door to a woman named Margaret Maxwell, who kept a small shop. They had owed the woman some money, and she had refused to give them further goods on credit. Out of revenge, the prisoners, during the evening of 16th February, broke into the house by the back window, pulled the woman from her bed, and smashed her skull to pieces. It was found that a silver watch, about £3 in money, and a copy of the New Testament, had been stolen. The two brothers were arrested, along with another labourer, Thomas M'Manes. The latter was not put on trial, but gave evidence that he was with the Scanlans when the crime took place.

The men were found guilty, and were sentenced to be hanged at Cupar on the 5th July. During the trial, the prisoners had remained perfectly still, but when sentence was passed they both shouted that they were innocent, and that the judges and jury were "d—— asses." On the 1st July a supplement to the death warrant was issued on account of the prison of Cupar being outwith the jurisdiction of the Cupar Magistrates. The warrant ordained the keeper of the prison to deliver the condemned men to the Sheriff of Fife, who in turn was to deliver them over to the Magistrates of Cupar, "for the purpose of seeing the death warrant carried out." The warrant further ordained the Sheriff to see the bodies buried within the precincts of the prison of Cupar, "as they all shall severally answer at their highest peril." A petition for a reprieve was refused.

A scaffold was borrowed from Edinburgh, and Calcraft, the celebrated London executioner, was engaged. The scaffold was erected at the north-east corner of the Fluthers Green, near Braehead, about six hundred yards from the prison. Dressed in the same white moleskin clothes which they had worn at the trial, the men were driven by omnibus from the jail (now a seed warehouse), Calcraft sitting next to one of his victims, while Bishop Gillies and a priest were also present. The Sheriff and police officials brought up the rear. On account of a rumour that a number of Irishmen from Dundee and labourers from the lime works would combine to rescue their comrades even from the clutches of Calcraft, extensive preparations were made by the authorities. Four hundred citizens were sworn in as special constables, while every available member of the County Police Force was drafted into the town. A strong detachment of the 42nd Regiment and the 7th Hussars from Piershill were also present. The prisoners kissed each other several times on the scaffold, and declared: "We are dying innocent of the murder of Margaret Maxwell, and forgive all who have to do with it"—meaning the witnesses at the trial. In front of the scaffold a woman, said to be the sweetheart of one of the brothers, was waving her hands and crying piteously. That brought forth the homely ejaculation from one of the men: "Peter, that's Marget."

The execution was carried through without a hitch, the overwhelming forces of law and order being more than sufficient to cope with any emergency. As the drop fell, a terrible thunderstorm broke over Cupar, which to a large extent cleared the streets of the thousands who had flocked into the town. Every place around the scaffold was densely crowded, and all the points of vantage which afforded a view of the dismal scene were occupied.

It has been said that this was "one of the day of days in Cupar's long history." All the roads had been crowded by break of day with carts conveying sightseers, far in excess of an ordinary fair. The writer has conversed with one who as a boy had been present at the execution. He said that he never saw such a large crowd of people in Cupar in all his life. Calcraft's fee was £30.

[The house where the murder took place has been removed, and the ground on which it stood now forms part of a field on the farm of Hilton of Forthar. The late Chief Constable Tennant-Gordon made special inquiries as to the exact "locus" of the house.]

December 23. Before the High Court of Justiciary at Edinburgh, George Christie was convicted of a murder near Kittybrewster, and was sentenced to be hanged at Aberdeen on the 13th January. The crime for which Christie forfeited his life was peculiarly brutal. His victims were Barbara Ross and her grandchild, about five years of age. Sunnybank, near Kittybrewster, was the scene of the tragedy. Christie had been employed on farm work near at hand, and was aware the woman would have some money in her possession, as she had sold two pigs. Returning from Aberdeen in a state of intoxication, he accomplished his foul deed with an axe, the floor of her room veritably running with blood. The prisoner denied the crime, but was identified as having been in the house of the deceased, and was also found to have some articles of the murdered woman in his possession.

When asked on the scaffold if he had anything to say, Christie calmly replied " No." He exhibited great fortitude at the closing scene. Calcraft was the executioner. Over 8,000 persons surrounded the scaffold, which was erected in front of the Town House in Castle Street.

1853.

February 21. Before the High Court of Justiciary at Edinburgh, the Lord Justice-Clerk and Lords Cowan and Anderson on the Bench, John Williams was sentenced to death for the murder of Andrew Mill, toll-keeper, at Cleek-him-in Toll, near Lauder. Williams was hanged at Greenlaw on the 12th March. The execution took place in front of the County Buildings (now disused). The scaffold was borrowed from Edinburgh, and Calcraft officiated. Pursuant to the sentence, the body was buried within

Greenlaw Prison. This was the last execution in Greenlaw, and also in Berwickshire.

August 11. Hans Smith M'Farlane and Helen Blackwood were hanged at Glasgow for the murder of Alexander Boyd, a ship's carpenter, by throwing him over a window in the New Vennel, Glasgow. Inveigled to the house, they had drugged Boyd with whisky and snuff, which rendered him insensible. Another woman, Ann Marshall, had also been convicted at the trial in Edinburgh of being concerned with the murder, but the sentence was commuted to transportation.

The principal witnesses for the prosecution were two little brothers, named Shillingshaw, both under the age of twelve years. They had slept under the bed in the house occupied by M'Farlane, and had watched the man being robbed and thrown over the window. As the boys had no home, they had been confined in prison since the tragedy. When sentenced, the woman exclaimed: "We have not got justice. There is a higher Judge for us. We are innocent."

After their removal from Edinburgh, M'Farlane made a request to the Governor of the North Prison (Duke Street) that he might be allowed to marry the woman. The request, however, was refused. Early on the morning of the day fixed for the execution, the prisoners were removed to the South Prison at the Green, where the final scene took place. M'Farlane was determined, however, to carry out his plan of marriage, which said much for him. Never was a celebration of union performed under such grim circumstances. Standing in front of the crowd—extending far away back to the Green, and numbering over 40,000 persons— M'Farlane in a firm voice said: "Helen Blackwood, before God and in the presence of these witnesses, I take you to be my wife. Do you consent?" "I do," replied the woman. "Then," continued the man, "before these witnesses I declare you to be what you have always been to me, a true and faithful wife, and you die an honest woman." "Amen," said the clergyman. A moment later the bolt was drawn. Born in the Calton district of Glasgow, M'Farlane could neither read nor write.

[This marriage, we understand, was not recorded in the Registrar General's book.]

1854.

April 19. At Ayr Circuit Court, Alexander Cunningham (35) was convicted of the murder of his wife, at Girvan, on the night of the Fast Day, 22nd December, 1853. Cunningham, who had been living apart from his wife, had shot her while at work at her loom in a weaver's shop. It was done deliberately and intentionally, for in order to get her into line with the shot he threw some gravel at the window to make her turn round. A moment later she was dead.

Lord Cockburn passed sentence of death, to be carried out at Ayr on the 11th May. A crowd of over 3,000 persons witnessed the execution. Calcraft was the hangman.

[This was the last person hanged at Ayr, and as the prison has now been demolished, no further executions can take place there. (See 1908).

An unprecedented situation arose in connection with the trial, as Lord Cockburn passed away on the 26th April, at his residence, Bonally, Midlothian, fifteen days before Cunningham was executed. Lord Cockburn describes the case in his "Circuit Journeys," and defines the panel as "a strong, resolute, dogged scoundrel."]

1857.

January 12. Before the High Court of Justiciary at Edinburgh, the Lord Justice-Clerk and Lords Cowan and Deas on the Bench, Peter M'Lean, a miner, and his wife, along with another man named William Mansfield, were charged with murdering and assaulting Thomas Maxwell, also a miner. They all belonged to Durhamston, near Bathgate. The crime took place on the public road, late on Saturday night, the 15th November, or early in the following morning. Sectarian strife was the cause of the trouble. Both parties were in a state of intoxication, and a disturbance had ensued between them. The fatal injuries were caused with a stone and a clasp knife.

The Solicitor-General, who prosecuted, asked for a conviction against the three prisoners, as they were each and all abetting in the violence. M'Lean was found guilty by a majority, but was recommended to the mercy and consideration of the Crown.

Mansfield was found guilty only of assault, and the charge against the woman not proven. M'Lean was sentenced to be hanged at Linlithgow on Monday, 2nd February, while Mansfield received sentence of two years' imprisonment. A reprieve was refused, and M'Lean duly paid the penalty in front of the County Hall.

Great excitement prevailed in the town, as thirty-eight years had passed since there had been an execution—Woodness, in 1819. Elaborate preparations were made for the carrying out of the sentence. Calcraft arrived several days previous to supervise the arrangements, but in case of illness or other causes, the Magistrates, no doubt mindful of the Court's injunction, "if the sentence was not carried out they would have to answer at their higher peril," another man, named Peddie, who came from Dundee, was engaged as assistant. A difficulty at first presented itself to the Magistrates. M'Lean was confined in the new prison, which is a considerable distance from the usual place of execution. It was considered that it would be illegal to remove him before eight o'clock on the morning of the day mentioned in the death warrant. It was thus deemed essential to secure the services of the 5th Dragoons from Piershill Barracks, on account of the dense crowd which would inevitably assemble. The Dragoons duly arrived, but at the same time an intimation was received from the Lord Advocate authorising the convict's removal to the old prison in the Square, adjoining the County Hall. The night previous to the execution, the condemned man was formally handed over to the Magistrates by the Governor of the Prison. The removal was effected shortly after ten o'clock on Sunday night. Escorted by a small body of police, M'Lean was taken to the old buildings and lodged in the only cell which remained.

Early on Monday morning, a party of carpenters arrived from Edinburgh with the scaffold, which had been borrowed from the Magistrates. Ten city constables were drafted from Edinburgh to aid the local force, while 250 special constables were sworn in, who guarded the barriers surrounding the scaffold. All the workmen at Kenneil Iron Works took a holiday for the occasion and thronged into the town. M'Lean, according to custom, addressed the crowd. In a trembling voice he said: "Good people, take warning by me. Avoid evil company and drink, and keep the Sabbath." The bolt was drawn, and in a few minutes the wretched man ceased to exist.*

June 30—July 7. Before the High Court of Justiciary at Edinburgh, the Lord Justice-Clerk (Hope) and Lords Handyside and Ivory on the Bench, Madeleine Hamilton Smith (21) was charged with the murder of her erstwhile lover, Pierre Emile L'Angelier, a native of Jersey. Miss Smith was a daughter of a well-known Glasgow architect, and moved in good society. There were three charges libelled in the indictment of administering arsenic between the 19th February and the 23rd March, at or near 7 Blytheswood Square, Glasgow,† where she resided with her father.

An imposing array of talent appeared both for the Crown and for the defence. The Lord-Advocate (Moncreiff), afterwards Lord Justice-Clerk; the Solicitor-General (Maitland), afterwards Lord Dundrennan, with Mr. Donald M'Kenzie, Advocate-Depute, appeared for the Crown. The Dean of Faculty (Inglis), afterwards the great Lord President; Mr. George Young, afterwards Lord Young, and Mr. A. Moncrieff, Advocate, conducted the defence.

The prisoner entered the dock, as it has been described by a reporter present, "with the air of a belle entering a ballroom or a box at the opera. Her steps were buoyant, and she carried a silver-topped bottle of smelling salts. She was stylishly dressed, and wore a pair of lavender gloves." Truly this was in striking contrast with the usual occupants of the dock.

L'Angelier, who had been employed in a warehouse in the city, had died suddenly, on the 23rd March, at his lodgings, 11 Franklin Place, Great Western Road. A *post-mortem* was made at the instigation of the firm by whom he was employed, and the report was forwarded to the police. Meantime the body was interred in the historic Ramshorn Churchyard (St. David's),‡ but the Crown ordered the body to be exhumed. It was subjected

---

*M'Lean's grave was marked by an arrow on the west wall of the prison, now dismantled.

† The house is now occupied by the Agricultural College.

‡ He was buried in the Fleming-Kennedy ground, not far from the entrance. His name, however, does not appear on the stone.

to a searching examination, which resulted in the recovery of no
less than thirty grains of arsenic.

There were over one hundred productions—letters, books,
prints, etc.—which all too plainly testified to illicit intercourse
having been carried on between them. In some of the letters the
prisoner concluded with the words: " Wifie mine." In one she
wrote: " Am I not your wife? Yes, I am." There was certainly
good ground, according to the letters, to make L'Angelier believe
that they were married according to Scots Law. Her attention
towards L'Angelier, however, began to cool, possibly in view of
a fresh suitor to her hand. This was a Mr. Minnoch, who was
of higher social position than the deceased, and to whom she
became formally engaged on the 28th January. She wished the
liaison, which had gone on for several months, terminated, and
asked for a return of the incriminating love letters. L'Angelier
pointedly refused to comply with this request, and even threatened
to lay them before her father, and Mr. Minnoch, who had ousted
him from her affections. To pacify L'Angelier, she once more
consented to keep company with him, and denied that her love
had turned towards another. There may, however, have been
good reason for this supposed reconciliation, which took place
about the 11th February. His nocturnal visits were renewed, but
twice after them the deceased was seized with an inexplicable
illness after having partaken of a cup of cocoa from her hands.
On his last alleged visit, there was no distinct evidence that he
kept the appointment on that Sunday evening, but police witnesses
testified that he was seen about ten o'clock that evening proceeding
in the direction of the prisoner's house. Between two and three
o'clock next morning, L'Angelier was found in a doubled-up
position at the door of his lodgings. He was carried into the house,
and although every attention was paid to him by his landlady and
Dr. Steven, he passed away at noon—not before recapitulating
his experiences of the two former attacks he had suffered.

Evidence was led on both sides at great length. Over eighty
witnesses in all were examined. The prisoner stated, in her
declaration, that she had not seen L'Angelier for three weeks
previous to his death. She affirmed that the poison she had
obtained on the pretext of killing vermin was used by her as a

cosmetic, and was diluted with water to wash her face, arms and neck. The Lord-Advocate addressed the jury on the seventh day of the trial, and claimed that they had no alternative but to find the prisoner guilty of murder as libelled, as there was ample motive disclosed to get L'Angelier out of the way. On the following day, the Dean of Faculty spoke on behalf of the prisoner. He began his address to the jury in these words: "Gentlemen of the jury, the charge against the prisoner is murder, and the punishment for murder is death, and that simple statement is sufficient to suggest to us the awful solemnity of the occasion which brings you and me face to face." He described the speech of the Lord-Advocate as one of great moderation: "Such moderation as I think must have convinced you that he could hardly have expected a verdict at your hands, and in the course of that address, for which I give him the highest credit, he could not resist the expression of his deep feeling of commiseration for the position in which the prisoner is placed." The Dean maintained there was no evidence that they ever met on the 21st February, nor on the Sunday in question. He suggested the possibility of suicide. The closing sentences of his brilliant forensic address were: "I am deeply conscious of a personal interest in your verdict, for should there be any failure of justice, I would attribute it to no other cause than my own inability to conduct the defence."

The Lord Justice-Clerk then summed up, which was continued on the following day—the ninth of the trial. The Court met one hour earlier than usual, at nine o'clock. His Lordship's charge was not unfavourable to the accused. In a densely crowded Court, the jury retired at five minutes past one o'clock. They were only absent half-an-hour, when Mr. Moffat, a High School master and foreman of the jury, announced "a verdict of not guilty of the first charge by a majority, of the second charge not proven, and by a majority find the third charge also not proven." The Lord Justice-Clerk added his concurrence to the verdict, which was highly popular. Great applause greeted the result. Madeleine Smith thus went free.

It has been remarked that none of her family came to the proceedings to give her succour and support in her time of need. One writer says the family took to their beds over the trial.

During the absence of the jury it was said that the least excited person in Court was the prisoner. Indeed, throughout the long, dreary hours she did not seem the least perturbed, and the fascinating and winsome manner of the small and dainty lady created quite a favourable impression. Who can deny that these qualities in no small manner contributed much to her acquittal? After all a judge and jury are only human!

[This trial stands out, if not the most noteworthy murder trial, at least as one of the three important murder trials that were investigated in Scotland last century, the others being the M'Lachlan and Monson cases. The country was then in the throes of an election, but it was not the oratory of the candidates that was engaging universal public attention. All eyes were focussed on the youthful figure in the dock. Before leaving the court, it was said that she received several offers of marriage. Inglis's noble peroration has become historic, and on several occasions since, a counsel defending a prisoner for murder has employed his opening sentences: "Gentlemen, the charge against the prisoner is murder, and the punishment for murder is death."

Madeleine Smith, some time after the trial, married a gentleman of good social position in London. Later she went abroad, and married again, and her death was announced in America on the 18th April, 1928. There were no children of the unions. The writer has in his possession a letter written by Madeleine Smith to Miss Aitken, the prison matron, in which she states she had several hundred letters, "all from gentlemen, some offering consolation and some their hearts and money."

The following appeared in a paper some years ago, and is given for what it is worth. A close friend of the Smith family, who was dining with them the day of L'Angelier's death, relates a dramatic story regarding the young lady. When at dinner he noticed that she kept her hands hidden under the table. Her habit was to display them openly, as they were unusually beautiful, and the omission to do so set him wondering. Afterwards he had an opportunity to view them at close quarters, when he found them stained with a blue substance. During the trial it was said the vermin exterminator alleged to have killed the deceased was a blue compound, denoting its poisonous character. This would probably have discoloured any tissues having contact with it. The friend kept his knowledge to himself, but had he mentioned the occurrence before the trial it might have changed the issue.]

September 24. At Aberdeen Circuit Court, before the Lord Justice-Clerk (Hope) and Lord Deas, John Booth (37), a travelling hawker, was found guilty of the murder of his mother-in-law, at Old Meldrum, on the 21st July. He had returned somewhat intoxicated, and charged his wife with infidelity. She ran out and took refuge in her mother's house, where she was followed by Booth. On his progress being barred by his mother-in-law, he inflicted fatal injuries with a knife. Booth had pleaded guilty to culpable homicide, but this was not accepted by the Crown. Sentence of death was passed, to take effect at Aberdeen, on the 21st October. The scaffold was erected in Castle Street, opposite the East Prison (now demolished). Booth, in a long speech, acknowledged the justice of his sentence. Calcraft was the hangman.

[This was the last person to suffer death at Aberdeen.]

December 22—24. At Glasgow Circuit Court, John Thomson, alias Peter Walker, was convicted of the murder of Agnes Montgomery, by administering prussic acid in beer at her house at Eaglesham, on the 13th September. There was also another charge of attempt to murder by a similar method. Agnes Montgomery, who was a mill worker, lived alone. Thomson had taken a fancy to her, but the affection was not returned. He therefore swore that she would suffer for it. Prussic acid as a poison had been much before the public in the recent Madeleine Smith case, and Thomson resolved to get some. A carrier's boy was commissioned to take "a line" to a drug store in Glasgow, and sixpence worth was procured, purporting to be for a portrait painter, Thomson instructing the boy to say nothing of the purchase. Several days later, on Sunday, the 13th September, the accused visited the house of the deceased. A neighbour spoke to hearing a terrible crash, and a few minutes afterwards she saw the prisoner leave and lock the door. When admittance was gained to the house, the woman was found speechless, and suffering great agony.

Thomson left Eaglesham and walked to Glasgow. On the way

he bought a bottle of whisky, and resolved that he would call at the house of Mr. and Mrs. Mason, St. John Street, where he had once lodged. After partaking of some refreshment from the bottle, Mason declared that it had a bad taste, while his wife said that after tasting some of the liquid she felt dizzy and saw "double," as she termed it. The police were informed, and Thomson was arrested.

Agnes Montgomery succumbed a few hours after the prisoner had left. The talk of a little girl to her mother as to what she had seen when playing about the doors when Thomson arrived at the house, and the other circumstances already mentioned, led to the authorities having the body exhumed. Medical witnesses on exhumation were of the opinion she had died from poison.

The Lord Justice-Clerk (Hope), in his charge to the jury, said the case was very peculiar, and there had been a great deal of theory. His Lordship said that man does not know the depravity or malignity of the human heart, and a number of criminals would escape because one could not understand what had led them to the commission of their crimes. "Suicide," continued the judge, "was out of the question, and the prisoner was the last to see her alive." After an absence of ten minutes the jury found the charge of murder proved. Sentence of death was passed, to be carried out at Paisley, on the 14th January.

Thomson, when led out to the drop, seemed quite dazed, and was attended by three clergymen. Although the morning was cold and stormy, yet large crowds gathered around the scaffold. When Calcraft pulled the lever, a number of men and women directly in front of the drop fainted with fright, and added much to the grimness of the proceedings. The groanings and yellings of the crowd could be heard a mile away. Thomson confessed that when only nine years of age he had drowned a boy, who was playing with him at Tarbert, by pushing him into a quarry.

1860.

December 17. Before the High Court of Justiciary at Edinburgh, Margaret Hannah was convicted of the murder of her infant child, at Old Luce, Wigtown, on the 6th August. The Lord

Justice-Clerk (Inglis) passed sentence of death, to be carried out at Stranraer, on the 6th January. Sentence commuted.

[This case is mentioned by Mr. Crabb Watt in his "Life of Lord President Inglis," but he there states that the charge was found not proven, and also that the crime took place in Ayrshire.]

December 27 and 28. At Glasgow Circuit Court, before Lord Ivory, Patrick Lunnay was found guilty of the murder of a man by stabbing him in a lodging-house at Alexandria, on the 11th November. Both men were under the influence of drink at the time. He was sentenced to be hanged at Dumbarton on the 16th January.

Lunnay, who was a Roman Catholic, was attended on the scaffold by Bishop Murdoch, from Glasgow. The condemned man met his fate, it is said, with "callous indifference," and affirmed that he was not guilty. A crowd numbering about 2,500 witnessed the execution, which took place in front of the County Buildings.

1862.

April 8. At Dumfries Circuit Court, before Lord Deas, Mary Reid or Timney was convicted of the murder of a quarrelsome neighbour, Ann Hannah, at Carsphairn, Parish of Kells, a small farm in the Stewartry of Kirkcudbright, on the 13th January. She inflicted the fatal injuries with a clothes beetle, but maintained that it was the deceased that struck her first. Great efforts were made in Dumfries—especially by two local ladies, who even visited Sir George Grey, the Home Secretary, at his seat in Northumberland—with a view of getting the sentence commuted, but this proved unsuccessful. It is believed that the attempt she made to incriminate her mother had told against her.

Mary Timney was hanged in public at Dumfries, amidst a peculiarly distressing scene. On the scaffold she repeatedly shrieked that mercy should be extended to her on account of her "four weans." She seemed to be completely paralysed, and had to be lifted up the steps to the scaffold, and was supported on each side. Just a minute before the bolt was drawn, considerable excitement was caused by a letter being hurriedly handed to the Prison Governor. Unfortunately the hopes of a reprieve

which were awakened proved false, as the letter was only from
a London newspaper, asking the Governor to wire an account of
the execution. The proceedings, which had been momentarily
suspended, then continued. A crowd, estimated at about 3,000
persons, surrounded the scaffold, which had been borrowed from
Edinburgh. The total expense of the execution was £100, in
addition to Calcraft's fee of £20 and expenses. Lord Deas came
in for considerable harsh criticism when the law was allowed to
take its course.

September 16—19. At Glasgow Circuit Court, before Lord
Deas, Jessie M'Intosh or M'Lachlan (28), wife of a seaman,
residing at the Broomielaw, was charged with the murder of an
acquaintance, Jessie M'Pherson, on the night of the 4th-5th July.
The murdered woman was a domestic servant employed by Mr.
John Fleming, 17 Sandyford Place, Glasgow. There was also a
charge of theft libelled. The prisoner, who had been at one time
a servant in the house, pleaded not guilty, and that specially the
crime was committed by Mr. James Fleming, 87 years of age,
who resided with his son, Mr. John Fleming. The murder was
not discovered until the return of Mr. John Fleming and his son
from a holiday, on the afternoon of Monday, 7th July. The old
man informed them that he had not seen "Jess," as he called
her, since Friday evening. On the Saturday morning she had not
brought up porridge as usual from the kitchen, situated in the
basement of the house. When she did not appear he tried her
bedroom door, but found it locked. He did not raise the alarm,
thinking that she had probably gone out to visit friends, and that
"Jess" would soon return. Throughout the whole week-end he
had cooked his own food, and also had attended Church on Sunday.

Mr. John Fleming proceeded to make investigation, and with
the aid of a pantry key succeeded in effecting an entrance to the
bedroom, the blinds of which were drawn. Entering the darkened
room, he was horrified to find the body of the servant lying on
the floor almost naked. A cloth had been flung across part of
the body. A chest belonging to the dead woman had been forced
open and some of the contents were strewn on the floor. A doctor
and the police were at once sent for. The former on examination

was of the opinion that death had taken place three days previous, and had resulted from injuries to the head and neck inflicted with great violence by a cleaver or some similar weapon. The body seemed to have been dragged from the kitchen face downward through the passage to her bedroom. The doctor also found the imprints of a woman's foot on blood in the passage, and it was apparent the kitchen floor had been recently washed. Two cleavers were found, one of which had been newly cleaned, and it seemed evident that this was the weapon used.

On searching the house it was discovered that a considerable amount of silver plate had been stolen. When old Mr. Fleming was interrogated by the police, he was asked if he had heard anything unusual on the previous Friday evening. He replied that he had heard a squeal in the early hours of Saturday morning and jumped out of bed to see the time. Two fainter squeals followed, but he returned to bed thinking that the noises came from a vacant piece of ground near at hand, where loose characters often congregated. The finger of suspicion seemed to point to old Mr. Fleming and he was arrested, but a different complexion was given to the case when some of the stolen articles were discovered in a pawnshop, where they had been pledged for £6 15/- by M'Lachlan, under the assumed name of Mary M'Donald.

The case presented some very unusual aspects, and it was not without apparent good cause that the police at first sought to connect the old man with the crime, but later it came to their knowledge that Mrs. M'Lachlan had been near the house. This fact and the pledging of the goods led to her arrest along with her husband. The latter was, however, immediately liberated, as he was able to satisfy the authorities that he had sailed on the steamer "Pladda" the day before the murder.

It was proved that Mrs. M'Lachlan had been in need of money, and that after the tragedy she was able to redeem articles which she had formerly pledged. As robbery seemed to have been the motive of the crime, old Mr. Fleming was liberated and Mrs. M'Lachlan committed for trial. She made three declarations, in which she stated that the old man was requiring money to take a holiday in the Highlands, and it was at his instigation that the silver plate was pledged. This statement, however, was discounted

F

by the fact that Mr. Fleming had about £200 standing to his credit at different banks. Indeed, the greater part of Mrs. M'Lachlan's story was found to be mere fabrication.

Mr. Adam Gifford, Advocate-Depute, conducted the case for the Crown, while Mr. Rutherfurd-Clark appeared for the defence. Evidence was led at considerable length. When old Mr. Fleming was cross-examined some sensational passages occurred. Several of his answers were in direct contradiction of the evidence he had already tendered. Here is an example. Mr. Rutherfurd-Clark: " When the milk came on Saturday, why did you not let Jessie open the door? " Mr. Fleming: " Ye ken it was a' ower wi' Jessie afore that." (Sensation in Court). But in the main the old man held to his story in most of the details he had already given the police, which was no doubt a remarkable achievement for a man of his age. The evidence, although purely circumstantial, was complete, having been linked together by Mr. M'Call, long the astute head of the detective department.

Mr. Adam Gifford, in addressing the jury, said there was sufficient evidence to convict the prisoner. " You will weigh everything upon evidence and leave nothing to be determined without proof," continued Mr. Gifford. The speech of Mr. Rutherfurd-Clark, which was received with great applause, was delivered with much skill and address.

Lord Deas's charge, which took four hours to deliver, was to a large extent one-sided, and was condemned by the majority of the newspapers and the general public as virtually another speech for the prosecution. But the " Glasgow Herald " was one of the exceptions. It had from the first taken up the position that Mrs. M'Lachlan was guilty and that Mr. Fleming was completely innocent. The jury were absent for only fifteen minutes considering their verdict when they unanimously found both charges proved.

Throughout the whole trial Jessie M'Lachlan, who seemed possessed of an iron nerve, sat in the dock calm and fearless. She now stood up, and throwing back her veil, said in a distinct voice: " I desire to have a statement read; I am as innocent as my child, who is only three years old this day." Mr. Rutherfurd-Clark then read a long document, perhaps the most remarkable

that was ever read in a Court of Justice. This associated Mr.
Fleming with the deed. The prisoner said that she was sent out
for drink when the murder took place, and was sworn to secrecy
on a large Bible by Mr. Fleming, while the goods had been
pawned for the purpose of making it appear the house had been
robbed.

Lord Deas, in passing sentence, described the statement as
"a tissue of wicked falsehoods." He sternly rebuked the prisoner
for endeavouring to implicate the old man, as there was not a
shadow of suspicion that he had anything to do with the crime.
Sentence of death was passed, to take effect on the 11th October.
As Lord Deas uttered the words, "May the Lord have mercy
on your soul," the prisoner exclaimed, "Mercy; aye, He'll have
mercy, for I am innocent." The panel was then r'moved, and
so concluded this remarkable trial.

Great controversy now ensued in the press and among the
public as to whether the facts brought forward were sufficient to
warrant a conviction. The jury were called together by the foreman and had a long conference in the Clarence Hotel. Fourteen
of the members were, however, of the opinion that there was no
ground for altering their verdict. A petition was prepared for
the Home Secretary, praying for a respite of the capital sentence,
which contained no fewer than 100,000 signatures. Yielding to
popular clamour the Crown took the unusual course of ordering a
supplementary inquiry, which was conducted by Mr. Young,
advocate, afterwards Lord Young. The case also formed the
subject of an elaborate debate in the House of Commons. But
neither the Commissioner's Report nor the debate before the
House lessened or removed the strange uncertainty and mystery
of the case.

A respite was subsequently granted until the 1st November,
when it was followed six days later by a communication commuting
the sentence to penal servitude for life. When the prisoner was
informed of the message she did not at once seem to comprehend
its full meaning, and said: "Then am I tae be kept in jail all
my days?"

[Sir Archibald Alison, who was at that time Sheriff of
Lanarkshire, has something of interest to say about the case

in his "Autobiography." He wrote a memorial for the Commissioner, and was strongly of opinion that the woman was innocent. "An accidental and constrained witness of the crime, but not an actor in it, except accessory to the murder after the fact." For months after the trial the case was the one absorbing topic of conversation, not only in Glasgow but throughout all Scotland. Lord Deas was generally censured by the public for his harsh summing-up against the prisoner, and so strongly upholding Mr. Fleming from any complicity with the crime.

So bitter was the feeling against Mr. Fleming that he was mobbed. Even doggerel verses were composed about him, and sung to a hymn tune by boys in the street:—

> " I wish I was in the land of Canaan,
>   Spinning ropes to hang old Fleming."

By the way, the metropolis of the event has always been noted for verses in connection with crime and the police. The following quatrain was common in the city sixty years ago:—

> " Corn rigs and barley rigs
>   Are kent through all the nation,
>   But the Candleriggs is nearest to
>   The Central Police Station."

Jessie M'Lachlan was liberated from Perth Penitentiary in October, 1877. She went to reside with her husband until his death in 1880. Afterwards she proceeded abroad, and was followed by her son. Jessie M'Lachlan married a second time, and died at Port Huron, Michigan, on the 1st January, 1899. A niece, who lived at Greenock, said that her aunt when liberated still affirmed her complete innocence, and said that it would all come right at the Judgment Day.

Mr. Fleming died exactly two years * after the trial. His tombstone, No. 134, can still be seen in the churchyard attached to Anderston Old Church, Glasgow.

The M'Lachlan case again came before the public in May, 1892, when a woman, Isabella M'Lennan or M'Gregor, on her deathbed at Dundee, confessed that she had committed the

---

* 16th September, 1864.

murder. She also stated that a box in her possession should be opened at her death. This was found to contain, among other things, several newspaper reports of the case. Speculation was again rekindled as to whether a grave injustice had not been done, but no real corroboration could be found of her tragic utterance. The police, both in Dundee and in Glasgow, were sceptical of the confession.

The late Mr. H. B. Irving, who was a great criminologist, said of the M'Lachlan case that it was the most absorbing which had ever engaged his attention. It was reported that when the jury retired to consider their verdict, after a chancellor or foreman was appointed, it was agreed that he should retire to a part of the room and that each member should deliver his opinion unknown to the others. All the fifteen jurors found the prisoner guilty.]

1863.

April 23. At Glasgow Circuit Court, before Lord Deas, John Reilly, or "Sodger" Reilly, as he was familiarly termed, was found guilty of the murder of a married woman for the purpose of robbery, on the public road between Holytown and Newhouse, Lanarkshire. Suspicion at first rested upon a miner, named Doyle, who was arrested, but he was soon liberated. A hue and cry was next raised against Reilly, who had disappeared two days after the murder. He was a labourer, and at one time had served with the 60th Rifles in India. Reilly was traced to Biggar and Hawick, but was at length arrested in Northumberland. The constable who arrested him deponed that the man at first confessed, but afterwards withdrew his statement. When sentenced he exclaimed: " You are condemning an innocent men."

Reilly was hanged in front of the South Prison of Glasgow, on the 16th May. He was attended on the scaffold by Bishop Murdoch, but contrary to the usual practice, did not address the crowd, which was estimated at over 30,000 persons.

1864.

May 29 and 30. Before the High Court of Justiciary at Edinburgh, the Lord Justice-General (M'Neil) presiding, and Lords

Neaves and Jerviswood on the Bench, George Bryce (30), a carter, was found guilty of the murder, on the 16th April, of a young woman, named Jane Seton, who was a nursery maid in a villa near Ratho. A servant in the same house had jilted him, and believing that this was brought about by Jane Seton, he made up his mind on revenge. Bryce forced his way into the villa of Seton's mistress, seized the girl and threw her down. Her screams brought, among others, the mistress, who struck him with an umbrella, which made him release his grip. His victim then got up and ran out of the villa, intending to take refuge in a cottage nearby. But before she could reach the door Bryce had overtaken her, and with a razor inflicted a frightful wound, which terminated fatally in a few minutes.

He was arrested in the evening, after an extensive search of the district had been made by the police, assisted by men from the surrounding quarries. A plea of insanity was put forward by the defence, but the jury, after an absence of a quarter of an hour, returned a verdict of guilty, but recommended him to mercy. Bryce was sentenced to be hanged on the 21st June. A reprieve was refused, and one morning, a few minutes after eight o'clock, the unhappy man duly paid the penalty at the usual place of execution in the city, at the head of Libberton's Wynd. He was removed from the Calton Jail to the cells below the High Court the night previous to the execution. Next morning he was escorted to a room in the County Buildings, where he was pinioned.

The late Superintendent Minty, of the Edinburgh Police, who was on duty, used to give a most vivid account of the grim proceedings. The procession moved up Libberton's Wynd (where the Midlothian County Buildings now stand), the scaffold being all the time in full view at the top of the slope. Under the scaffold a rough black coffin lay exposed. On Bryce taking his place on the drop, " The hour of my departure's come " was sung. Thereafter the condemned man gave the usual signal by dropping a handkerchief. A moment later the bolt was drawn; but the drop was too short, and three or four minutes elapsed before death fortunately supervened, all the while Bryce was raising his shoulders and wriggling at the end of the rope—a terrible sight.

An hour later, about nine o'clock, Dr. Henry Littlejohn (afterwards Sir Henry), the police surgeon, pronounced the man dead. The body was laid in the coffin without any ceremony, and the joiners made it fast. It was then placed in a cart and driven by a labourer in his ordinary clothes to the Calton Jail, and there buried.

The hangman was a convicted prisoner, Askern, of York, as his better known rival in the trade was otherwise engaged. Askern, who was over six feet in height and had bushy whiskers, was dressed in a velvet coat, corduroy knee breeches with leggings, and, according to Mr. Minty, looked like a rat catcher. "But we did not see a man like that go away," said the officer, as Askern adopted another dress for fear of the mob. Street singers and missionaries were much in evidence, and the latter improved the occasion by singing psalms, praying, and exhorting the crowd, which numbered about 20,000, to take warning by the solemn scene, which turned out to be the last public execution in the city.

[Curiously, James Bryce, a nephew of George Bryce, met a similar fate at the same place in 1844 for murder. The Ratho trial was noteworthy as being the last occasion the head of the Justiciary Court pronounced sentence of death. Lord President M'Neil had an unique record of Court attendance. During his fifteen years' service as a Lord-Ordinary and fourteen as head of the Court, he was only twice absent from the Court of Session; once while presiding at this trial in the High Court; the other occasion was when honoured with "a command" to Buckingham Palace. He was elevated to the House of Lords in February, 1867, in his 74th year, and adopted the title of Lord Colonsay. He was the first judge since the Union of Scotland and England to be raised to the Peerage. He had succeeded Lord President Boyle in 1852. Lord Colonsay died at Pau, in January, 1874, and was buried in the Warriston Cemetery, Edinburgh.

To all those who cross over the Forth Bridge, the cemetery at North Queensferry is familiar. A freestone cross at the top—which was the first monument erected there—has, curiously, no date, but bears the words:—

" Jane Seton, 23.

I know, O Lord, that thy judgments are right. Into thine
hands I commit my spirit. Thou hast redeemed me,
    O Lord, God of Truth.—Psalm XXXI., verse 5.
Erected by the children to whom she was a nurse,
        as a mark of love."

Jane Seton, who was a native of Queensferry, was the first
person buried in the cemetery.]

1865.

April 18 and 19. At Aberdeen Circuit Court, before the Lord
Justice-Clerk (Inglis) and Lord Cowan, George Stephen (62), a
wood merchant, pleaded guilty to the murder of a married woman,
named Forbes, at Thainstone Woods, on the 3rd December. His
counsel subsequently withdrew his plea of guilty, and intimated
the panel was insane at the time of the tragedy. His Lordship,
in the course of a discussion between the Crown and the defence
following the plea of guilty, said that evidence must be led, as it
was not according to custom, nor was it deemed expedient, to
award a capital sentence on the testimony of the accused himself.
Evidence was then led. Stephen was found guilty by a majority
of the jury, and sentence of death was passed, to be carried out
at Aberdeen on Wednesday, 17th May. Sentence commuted.

[The procedure adopted in Scotland when a plea of guilty is
tendered in a murder trial is thus in direct contrast with that in
England. There no evidence is led, the reading of the charge and
the passing of the sentence occupying about four minutes only.*
For the next instance in Scotland of a plea of guilty in a murder
charge, see case of Bone, at Glasgow, in 1908.]

July 3—7. Before the High Court of Justiciary at Edinburgh.
The Lord Justice-Clerk (Inglis) presided, with Lords Ardmillan
and Jerviswood. Edward William Pritchard, M.D., Glasgow, was
charged with the murder, by poisoning, of his wife and mother-
in-law, Mrs. Taylor, within his house, Clarence Place, 131

---

* Liverpool Assizes, before Mr. Justice Finlay. Charge against Reginald Victor
  Clark. From the time he entered the dock and left, 4¼ minutes only elapsed.

Sauchiehall Street, Glasgow, in the preceding February and March. On account of the Lord Advocate (Moncreiff) having been called to London on Parliamentary business, the Solicitor-General (Young) prosecuted. Mr. Rutherfurd-Clark was chief counsel for the defence.

Probably Pritchard's misdeeds might have gone unpunished had not an anonymous letter been sent to the Procurator-Fiscal on the death of Mrs. Pritchard, who had died in the same mysterious manner as Mrs. Taylor had done three weeks previous. Pritchard had been arrested at Queen Street Station, on returning from Edinburgh after the funeral of his wife, who was buried in the Grange Cemetery, Edinburgh, beside her mother. The bodies were subsequently exhumed. The stomach and other intestinal organs were subjected to chemical analysis.

Among the witnesses for the Crown was Mary M'Leod (17), a servant girl employed in the house. Dr. Pritchard and the girl had carried on an illicit intercourse for some time, and she disclosed that the prisoner had promised to marry her if Mrs. Pritchard died. She stated that she had also received presents from him. Dr. James Paterson was another important witness for the prosecution. It was he who was called to see Mrs. Pritchard by the prisoner, when he formed the impression that she was being slowly poisoned with antimony. When asked by the Registrar to certify the cause of death, he said that he believed she was under some narcotic but was not inclined to state the exact cause, but that Dr. Pritchard would give a satisfactory explanation. This statement was accepted by the Registrar.

In the witness box, and also during his Lordship's address to the jury, Dr. Paterson was censured for not divulging the information in time so that possibly a life would have been spared. A liferent of £2,500, for which he was curator for his children until they reached their majority, descended to Pritchard at his wife's death, and this was the only pecuniary gain the Crown could establish against him for the death of Mrs. Pritchard. Pritchard's children, a little girl of fourteen years of age, and a boy of eleven, were put into the witness box for the defence to prove the friendly relationship that existed between the parents. Three diaries of the prisoner were among the "productions." The entries had evidently been made in case there should be any inquiries into the deaths. They showed that truly he was an arch-hypocrite of the blackest hue. One cannot believe there is any parallel to the entries that he so cunningly put together. Here is one:—

" March, 1865. 17th, Friday.
Died here, at 1 a.m., my own beloved wife. Aged 38.

No torment surrounding her bedside, but like a calm and peaceful Lamb of God passed away Minnie. May God and Jesus, Holy Ghost, One in Three, welcome Minnie. Prayer on prayer till mine be o'er, everlasting love. Save us, Lord, for Thy dear Son."

The Solicitor-General, in addressing the jury, claimed that the two women had been poisoned by antimony and aconite. It was not suicide nor accident. Mary M'Leod was the only grown-up person in the house along with Pritchard, and there was not a shadow of suspicion that she had anything to do with the murder. " For," concluded Mr. Young, " it was murder with a doctor's finger in it." Mr. Rutherfurd-Clark, for the defence, said if the prisoner committed the crimes he was " one of the foulest criminals that ever lived." He next touched on the question of motive, which, according to the pecuniary gain, was slight, and it was not probable that Pritchard would ever think of marrying Mary M'Leod. Another point that stress was laid upon by the defence was that the servant was the only person who administered the food which had been poisoned, but there was no proof it was done by Pritchard.

Mr. Rutherfurd-Clark then spoke of the nerve of the prisoner, kneeling down and kissing Mrs. Pritchard while in death before her relatives—" those lips which his hand had closed, suppose such is the case. One would almost believe the thunderbolt of the Almighty would have stricken down the man who would have done it." In conclusion, the learned advocate asked for a verdict of acquittal, and to restore the prisoner to his orphaned family and sorrowing friends.

The Lord Justice-Clerk proceeded to sum up on Friday, the fifth day of the trial. It was plain from the outset that he thought the charges had been established. His Lordship said one could not imagine that a girl of seventeen years of age could have herself conceived and executed such a design, and if she had conceived, "could she have executed it within the house, under the eye and subjected to the vigilance of the husband of one of the victims, himself a medical man?" The jury retired to consider their verdict at 1.20 p.m., and after an absence of fifty-five minutes, returned and announced that they had unanimously found both charges proved. In passing sentence, his Lordship said: "The evidence leaves in the mind of no reasonable man the slightest doubt of your guilt." Sentence of death was passed, to be carried out at Glasgow, on the 28th July. Pritchard bowed to the bench and jury before leaving the dock. He was transmitted, "under sure guard" in terms of the sentence, to the North Prison (Duke Street) next day.

Pritchard made a series of confessions and freely acknowledged the justice of his sentence. He attributed his misdeeds "to a species of terrible madness and the use of ardent spirits." Pritchard was removed to the South Prison, opposite the Green, late on the evening prior to the execution. It was Fair time, and part of the Green had been filled with shows, booths, etc. They were, however, removed by order of the Magistrates, and barricades erected to relieve the pressure in view of a large crowd assembling. Despite a drizzling rain, a vast concourse of persons witnessed the execution.* Before ascending the scaffold, the condemned man in a firm voice said: "I acknowledge the justice of my sentence." He was attired in deep mourning, wearing the clothes in which he was apprehended after returning from his wife's funeral. Calcraft was cheered and hooted alternately, while a force of 750 constables maintained excellent order. The body was subsequently interred in the courtyard of the prison. That was the last public execution in Glasgow.

Pritchard was a member of nearly twenty learned societies in the kingdom, and was the author of "Filey as a Watering Place," "A Visit to the Pitcairn Islands," etc. He also contributed numerous articles to the medical press, and was a poet of no mean ability.

---

*A newspaper report said: "After the bolt was drawn he shrugged his shoulders more than half-a-dozen times, his head shook, and the whole body trembled."

[Great interest was taken in the proceedings. With the exception of the Madeleine Smith and M'Lachlan trials, this was the greatest *cause célébre* which had been investigated in Scotland for years. In some respects it bore a strong resemblance to the trial of William Palmer, in England, a decade earlier. Both men occupied good positions in the medical profession. Both administered poison. Palmer used strychnine, and Pritchard tartarised antimony and aconite. Both men were found guilty and both were hanged. Another singularity was that the venue of the trials was changed in both instances: Palmer from Stafford to the Central Criminal Court, London, in order to ensure an impartial verdict, public feeling in Staffordshire being very much against him. The Pritchard case, instead of coming up at the usual Circuit, was remitted to Edinburgh for trial.

Dr. Paterson, one of the witnesses already mentioned, took the unusual course of replying to the severe castigation he had received from the Bench through the medium of the Press. In this he stated that if his private opinion had not been borne out, he might have been liable to an action for damages, and he did not wish to take the risk. His friends in Glasgow, as a mark of sympathy, presented him with a testimonial to the effect that he had discharged his duty as a physician and a citizen under specially trying circumstances.

After the trial, some attempt was made to connect Pritchard with a fire which occurred at his house in May, 1863, when a servant girl was burned to death. Her charred remains were all that was found. It was thought that he committed the deed to hide his shame.

The burial place of Pritchard's wife and mother-in-law, in the Grange Cemetery, Edinburgh, is even after all these years still an object of morbid interest. It can easily be found, as it is the second stone from the entrance next to Lovers' Lane. Two copper beeches stand sentinel over the grave.

As it has been said, Pritchard courted the Muse to good effect, and the following verses, greeting the New Year (1862), are from his diary, written at Berkeley Terrace: —

" Arise in splendour, magnificent to view,
 One thousand, eight hundred and sixty-two;
Shed o'er the land a jovial, happy time;
 Send peace and plenty through every clime.
Uphold the right, the wrong dismay;
 Cheer on the useful, industrious, truthful day.
To him who here indites his little muse,
 Great Being, Commander of the Worlds,
Hold him, keep him, keep amidst Thy pearls;
 He looks to Thee, Thy Son his Friend—
Prosperity, peace, plenty, power to the end."

One might have thought that Pritchard's remains would rest in peace in the courtyard of classic Jail Square, but it was not so, for the remains of the murderers who had been buried there were removed in 1910, when the Justiciary Buildings were renovated. Little or no ceremony was observed at the work of exhumation and the bones of many victims of the law were tumbled into a herring box borrowed from the adjacent market, and buried elsewhere. When Pritchard's grave was opened, the skeleton was found to be well preserved, the skull,* teeth, and limbs were complete, elastic-sided boots were in good condition, while portions of mouldy garments could be observed.

Under a provision of the Habeas Corpus Act, of 1701, a prisoner could compel the Crown to serve an indictment within sixty days, a period known as "running his letters." A further period of forty days could be claimed only before the trial had to be concluded. On the 30th March, Pritchard's agents took advantage of this provision, and made intimation to the Crown. The period of "running his letters" expired on the 1st June, and the trial had thus to terminate before the 10th July, or else the prisoner could claim his freedom. On account of the difficulty of getting up the case, the Crown were not able to proceed with the trial before the 3rd July. Had the defence evinced a determination to protract the proceedings, the Court would have sat throughout the night, so as to conclude before the 10th July. As it was it terminated three days earlier.]

* See " Glasgow Medical Journal," 1912, page 104, for report of the examination of the skull.

1866.

January 8—10. Before the High Court of Justiciary at Edinburgh, the Lord Justice-Clerk (Inglis) and Lords Neaves and Ardmillan on the Bench, Andrew Brown (25), a seaman, was charged with the murder of John Greig, Jr., master of the schooner "Nymph," while off the coast of Forfarshire, on the 6th September, 1865. A special plea of insanity was intimated by the defence. The evidence showed the "Nymph" had left Montrose for London with a cargo of flooring. The schooner contained four men—John Greig, Jr., the master; Andrew Brown, and two other seamen, named Pert and Rae. When off Redhead, two and a half miles off the Forfarshire coast, Brown attacked the skipper with an axe, as he lay asleep, striking him two terrible blows on the head. Pert rushed at Brown and prevented him striking a third blow at the lifeless body. He also managed to take the axe from Brown and throw it overboard. Brown took command of the vessel, and said he would steer it to Stonehaven, where his mother lived, and if anyone disobeyed his commands he would be pitched overboard. He said he had killed the skipper on account of some former grudge. On the arrival of the schooner at Stonehaven, Brown proceeded to his mother's house, and the police having been informed, he was arrested there.

When Pert asked Brown on board the schooner what he had done, he replied: "Well, Jock, I am going stark mad, out of my mind." He also said: "Will you come and see me hanged? It is a good thing you got the axe, or you would have got the same." But this evidence did not satisfy the jury there was any weakness of mind. They retired at nine o'clock, and after an absence of nearly an hour, returned a unanimous verdict of guilty, while a minority added a recommendation to mercy.

Sentence was delayed until Wednesday morning, owing to the difficulty of finding a place for execution—whether it should be in Kincardineshire or Forfarshire. The diet having been called on the 10th January, the Lord Justice-Clerk passed sentence of death. Brown was ordained to be transmitted under sure guard to the prison of Forfar, there to be detained until the 31st day of January current, and upon that day to be taken forth of the said prison and transmitted under sure guard till brought to the Burgh of Montrose, and there, between the hours of two and four o'clock afternoon, in the common place of execution in that burgh, or at such other place in that burgh as the Magistrates of Montrose shall appoint, to be hanged by the neck on a gibbet. The body thereafter to be buried within the precincts of Forfar Prison.

During the passing of the sentence, Brown exhibited no emotion, and, it was reported, was not the least affected by his awful position. Sir George Gray, the Home Secretary, refused to grant any respite to the convict, saying that he agreed with the opinion of the Lord Justice-Clerk that the plea of insanity was an entire failure.

In terms of the sentence, Brown was removed by special train in the early hours of the morning from Forfar to Montrose, where he was incarcerated in the Police Office until the afternoon. The scaffold, which had been borrowed from Aberdeen, was erected in George Street, in front of the Police Office. Over 150 citizens were sworn in as special constables. Calcraft was the executioner. The crowd which surrounded the scaffold was estimated about 3,500, and was quiet and orderly. Calcraft left for the south shortly after the execution. He was escorted to the station by about forty constables, and was frequently hissed. The body of Brown was removed in the evening to Forfar, where it was interred under the direction of Sheriff Heriot.

The last previous execution at Montrose was that of Mrs. Shuttleworth, on the 8th December, 1822.

April 24 and 25. At Perth Circuit Court, before Lords Neaves and Ardmillan, Joseph Bell, a young Derbyshire potter, was charged with the murder of Alexander M'Ewan, a baker's vanman, near Vicars Bridge, Blairingone, Perthshire, on the 18th December previous. The evidence for the Crown was purely circumstantial. Bell, a noted poacher, was seen in the neighbourhood on the evening of the tragedy. He had borrowed a gun on the previous day, and was then penniless. The purchases he had made before he was arrested and the money found in his possession exactly coincided with the amount stolen, viz., £5 10/-. The crime savoured of the old-time highwayman. The dull December day drawing to a close, with Bell on the outlook for the lights of the approaching cart. He was cognisant of the time M'Ewan was due to pass. The vanman was subsequently discovered lying on the roadside, his head veritably riddled with pellets. He was still alive, but shortly afterwards breathed his last in a house at Blairingone to which he was carried.

Link by link the police succeeded in connecting the crime with Bell, who was arrested in a house in Tillicoultry the night after the murder. The boots worn by Bell exactly corresponded to the footprints at the scene of the tragedy. It was also through the footprints that a gun was discovered under the arch of Vicars Bridge, which crosses the Devon. The gun in question was proved to have been in possession of the prisoner. Another strong factor against him was his attempt to account for the money in his possession by stating that he had received it from a game-dealer in Dunfermline. All the game-dealers in the neighbourhood were produced by the Crown as witnesses, when they severally declared that they had no transactions with the prisoner, and in fact he was quite unknown to them. Other evidence showed that Bell had originally intended to rob a Kinross-shire farmer, who was known to pass that way periodically to collect money from a mill which he owned. A witness, named Wright, stated that Bell had asked him to hold the farmer's horse while he (Bell) "would damage and chuck him."

The jury, after an absence of twenty-five minutes, unanimously found Bell guilty. Lord Ardmillan, in passing sentence, said that although no human eye had seen the crime committed, he had been found guilty to the satisfaction of the jury, and that was always to the satisfaction of the law. His Lordship fixed the execution to take place at Perth, on the 22nd May, between the hours of eight and ten o'clock forenoon. When Lord Ardmillan had concluded, Bell ejaculated, "Thank you, my Lord, I am innocent."

There was no public petition to the Home Secretary to obtain a commutation of the sentence, but the prisoner's agent forwarded a petition on Bell's behalf, setting forth three points in his favour, one of which was that the judge had charged strongly in favour of acquittal. The petition, however, proved unavailing. Bell seemed quite indifferent to his fate, but strongly denied that he was guilty. He occupied most of his time in prison reading the Bible and writing poetry. The Rev. Mr. Milne, of the West Church, Perth, purchased, at the condemned man's request, a number of books to send to friends. On the title page he write his poetic effusion:—

> " Dear Father and Mother, it is the 12th of May,
> I wrote these lines for you to-day;
> Sad news they will have to tell,
> About our parting, Joseph Bell.
> In remembrance of me pray keep this book,
> With earnest eyes do on it look,
> For this day we must take farewell.
> Your loving son, Joseph Bell."

To his Uncle:—

> " I cannot help speaking without amaze;
> See how the Court did on the jury gaze;
> When the verdict of guilty did sound its knell,
> Upon your nephew, Joseph Bell."

The Chaplain of the Prison, the Rev. Mr. St. Clair, addressed a letter to the unfortunate man on the morning of his execution, exhorting him to confess. "In about ten or fifteen minutes you will be no more." But even this grave warning had not the desired effect, for Bell promptly wrote back the following reply:—

> " My dear Sir,
>> Pritchard confessed to his crime,
>> Because he was guilty of the crime.
> My dear Sir,
>> Joseph Bell is going to be executed to-day
>> for murder that he knows nothing about."

The scaffold, erected against the south wall of the prison, had been borrowed from Aberdeen. Just a moment before Calcraft drew the bolt, Bell maintained that he was innocent. A crowd, estimated at about 2,000, surrounded the barricades.

[The case naturally excited much local interest, and the tree

G

opposite the spot where the vanman was found has many initials
carved upon it. Situated on the left-hand side of the road, about
midway between the railway viaduct and Blairingone Mains, it
is still an object of morbid interest. On the day of the execution
a large number of villagers from the surrounding hamlets, and
from Kinross, trudged to the Fair City to see Joe Bell "swing
from the gallows tree."]

1867.

April 8. At Perth Circuit Court, before the Lord Justice-Clerk
(Glenalmond) and Lord Deas. The principal case before the Court
was the Mount Stuart murder charge. The accused was found
not guilty.

[The judges arrived in the city on Saturday, the 6th, and
put up at their usual "lodgings," the Royal George Hotel. On
Sunday they attended service in the East Church. A levee was
held before proceeding to the Court on the Monday, when the
present spacious Courtroom was inaugurated. The usual ceremonial procession took place to the Court. A company of the
4th Queen's Own Hussars acted as escort, while the procession
was led by the band of the 1st Perthshire Volunteer Rifles.]

December 16. Before the High Court of Justiciary at Edinburgh, the Lord Justice-Clerk (Glenalmond) and Lords Ardmillan
and Jerviswood on the Bench, Charles Macdonald (40), a tinker,
was convicted of the murder of his wife, during a drunken brawl
on the 28th September, near Deanshaugh Inn, on the road leading
from Amulree to Dunkeld. One of the witnesses for the Crown
was the son of the accused, twelve years of age, who like his
father could hardly read. He deponed that on previous occasions
the prisoner had repeatedly knocked his mother while in drink.
The boy was closely questioned by the judges if he knew what
it was to speak the truth. Here are two examples:—

Lord Jerviswood: "What religion does your father belong?"
Answer: "A flour miller." (Laughter).
Lord Ardmillan: "Have you been to school?" No answer.
Lord Ardmillan: "Hae ye been to ony schule?" (Laughter).
Answer: "Yes."

1868.

April 21. At Dumfries Circuit Court, before the Lord Justice-Clerk (Glenalmond), Robert Smith (19) was found guilty of the murder of a little girl, named Scott, near Cummertrees, Annan, on the 1st February. The case was peculiarly revolting. Smith, who had no fixed place of abode, robbed the girl of some money while on her way to Annan for messages. He had carried her into Kinmont Wood, and when she refused to hand over the money, robbed and criminally assaulted her. Fearing the consequences, he next strangled her with a bootlace.

Smith, who had remembered that he had been seen in the girl's company on the road to Annan by a Mrs. Crichton, who might possibly give evidence against him, resolved to turn back to her cottage, where he attempted to cut her throat with a large knife which he carried. Fortunately he was disturbed by the arrival of a neighbour, and at once took to his heels across the fields. When the little girl did not return, a search party was organised, and the body was discovered.

The outrage on Mrs. Crichton naturally increased the alarm, and throughout the night an extensive search was continued. It was supposed the man was still hiding in the woods. When the local congregation assembled next day, Sunday, they were dismissed by the minister in these words: " We can do no higher service to God this day than by doing what lies in our power to run to earth the cowardly assassin of the little member of our flock whom we all knew and loved so well."

Some sixty persons, a number of whom were on horseback, now augmented the police search party. But a little later in the day information was received that the man had been arrested by Sergeant Malcolm in a lodging-house in Dumfries while playing with an infant child. (The Sergeant was afterwards Chief Constable of the Burgh.)

As the Private Execution Act was only awaiting the Royal assent to become law, every effort was made by the Provost to have the final scene carried out within prison walls. This, however, was unsuccessful, and the scaffold was erected on its old stance, in Buccleuch Street, on the 12th May. Barricades surrounded the scaffold, which to some extent shut off from view the gruesome proceedings. The execution, which was the last public one in Scotland,* was, however, not carried through with dispatch, as the rope had to be taken off and readjusted before the bolt was drawn. Askern, of York, officiated.

[The last two executions in Dumfries were carried out in front of the prison erected in 1851. These were Mary Timney and Robert Smith. The prison, which stood where the Clydesdale Bank Buildings are now situated, fell into disuse in 1883, when the new prison at Maxwelltown was erected. An older prison, which stood also in Buccleuch Street, was the scene of six executions from 1807 to 1851. It was connected with the Court House on the opposite side of the street by an underground passage.]

1870.

September 7 and 8. At Perth Circuit Court, before the Lord Justice-Clerk (Moncreiff) and Lord Cowan, George Chalmers (45) was found guilty of the murder of John Miller, toll-keeper at Blackhill Toll Barr, near Braco, in December last. The case presented some unusual characteristics. Miller, who was unmarried, lived alone. He was last seen alive on the evening of the 21st December by a shepherd named M'Laren, while next morning he was found dead in the house with his head smashed. A blood-stained crowbar was lying by his side. It appears Miller had been struck down while preparing his supper. The house had been ransacked and some clothes taken away; a watch and some money were also missing, but several of the murderer's cast-off garments were found on the premises.

The local constable had a suspicion that he had seen a tramp wearing clothes which at least resembled those left. From inquiries it was learned that a tramp, named George Chalmers, who had undergone ten days' imprisonment for theft, had been liberated from Alloa Jail a day or so before the murder. A hue and cry was raised to find this man, who, it was supposed, had some connection with the tragedy.

Six months passed, and it was not until the following May that a Dundee constable came upon a man who answered the

*The last in England was Michael Barratt, at Newgate, on 26th May, 1868.

description of the much wanted Chalmers. He questioned him, but allowed the tramp to proceed along the Broughty Ferry Road. The constable reported the matter to his superior officers, and not being entirely satisfied with some of the man's answers, he resolved to follow him. He was going off duty, so putting on plain clothes the officer hurried away in the direction the tramp had taken. Some three miles out he came upon the object of his search sitting by the road side. After further interrogation, the man was arrested and charged with murder.

Chalmers admitted that he was the person who was imprisoned in Alloa, but denied that he had ever been near Braco. The fact, however, that he was wearing some of the toll-keeper's clothes told against him, while the discarded property left in the house was identified by the prison authorities as having belonged to Chalmers. The jury, by a majority of 13 to 2, found the prisoner guilty, and sentence of death was passed.

Chalmers was hanged within the walls of the now disused County Prison at Perth, on Tuesday, 4th October. Calcraft was the executioner. The condemned man protested his innocence to the end. His last words were: "Farewell for evermore; thank God I am innocent." This was the first private execution in Scotland.

1873.

April 8. At Dundee Circuit Court, before Lords Deas and Jerviswood, Thomas Scobbie was charged with the murder of a gamekeeper, at Kingennie, near Dundee, in September last.

Lord Deas summed up strongly against the prisoner. After an absence of ten minutes, the jury returned a verdict of guilty as libelled by a majority of 14 to 1, and by the same majority recommended the panel to mercy. Lord Deas passed sentence of death, to be carried out within Dundee Prison, on the 29th April.

[On account of the phraseology of the clerk, an error occurred in the record. The execution was fixed to take place on "Tuesday, 29th April next to come." As there was not a "Tuesday, 29th April next to come" for five years, it was considered the warrant could not be legally carried out.]

1874.

October 8 and 9. At Glasgow Circuit Court, before the Lord Justice-Clerk (Moncreiff)—(Old Court)—Archibald Miller was charged with the murder of his wife, in Glasgow. A special plea of insanity was put forward by the defence, which was conducted by Mr. Macdonald (afterwards Lord Kingsburgh). The jury, by a majority, found the prisoner guilty as libelled, and added "that he was of sound mind when the crime was committed." The verdict was received with great surprise, as the general opinion seemed to be Miller would be found insane. During the trial the prisoner never spoke to his counsel or agent, his demeanour being of the most stolid description. Sentence commuted.

[Sir J. H. A. Macdonald (Lord Kingsburgh), in his "Jottings," states that he successfully defended each charge of murder until the cases of the four poachers (see 1883 and 1884), but this trial must have escaped his memory.]

1875.

September 14. At Glasgow Circuit Court, before Lord Neaves—(New Court)—Patrick Docherty (21) was charged with the murder of a miner by striking him over the head with a hoe, near Rutherglen Bridge. He pleaded not guilty, and was defended by Mr. Thomas Shaw (the late Lord Craigmyle). Mr. J. P. B. Robertson (afterwards Lord Robertson of Forteviot) was Advocate-Depute. Evidence was led, and the charge was found proved. Sentence of death was passed, to be carried out within the South Prison of Glasgow, on the 5th October. Petitions were forwarded to the Home Secretary, praying for a reprieve, but they were refused, and Docherty duly paid the penalty.

[The evidence bore out that the deceased had met his death in something of the nature of a street brawl, and the attack was committed on the impulse of the moment.

Another man, named Middleby, was also convicted of murder at this Circuit. In this case the prisoner was of mature age, and the act was deliberately accomplished, while the weapon, a pick, inflicted terrible injuries to the head. The capital sentence was, however, commuted to penal servitude.

Some sections of the public believed that the cases had got mixed up while under review, and if the Royal clemency should have been extended to any, Pat Docherty's was undoubtedly the case which deserved it. John Bright, in Parliament, denounced the hanging of the lad as judicial murder.*]

September 16. At Glasgow Circuit Court, before Lord Ardmillan—(Old Court)—John Middleby or Tierney was found guilty of the murder of a miner, named Campbell, by inflicting fatal injuries to the head with a pick. The verdict was accompanied by a recommendation to mercy. Sentence commuted.

[See note to previous case.]

September 28. At Stirling Circuit Court, before Lords Ardmillan and Neaves, David Wardlaw, a shoemaker, was charged with the murder of his wife, at Bonhill, Dumbarton. The prisoner, a little old man, pleaded not guilty, and was defended by Mr. A. J. Young and Mr. Graham Murray (now the veteran Lord Dunedin). Lord Neaves summed up strongly against the prisoner. The jury returned a verdict of guilty as libelled, by a majority of 11 to 4, coupled with a unanimous recommendation to mercy on account of the dissipated habits of the deceased. Sentence of death was passed, to be carried out within Dumbarton Prison, on the 19th October.

Wardlaw stated that for twenty years there had been frequent quarrels with his wife, intoxication being mainly the cause. Three petitions were forwarded to the Home Secretary, craving for a respite; one from the inhabitants of the Vale of Leven, another from the jury, and thirdly, one from the Town Council and counsel attending the Western Circuit. Wardlaw, however, paid the last penalty.

[This was the last execution at Dumbarton, and also the last capital conviction at Stirling. The case synchronised with the opening of the new County Buildings, in place of the old quarters in Broad Street.]

1876.

May 10. At Glasgow Circuit Court, before the Lord Justice-Clerk—(Old Court)—Thomas Bass was charged with the murder

---

*" Letters to Isabel," by the late Lord Craigmyle.

of his wife and mother-in-law, Mrs. Sloan, in her house in the Gallowgate, Glasgow, on the 1st March. Bass, who had been a widower, had married again, but domestic trouble soon intervened. It was stated that his wife had left him on no fewer than seventeen occasions. On the last occasion the prisoner followed her to the house of Mrs. Sloan, who attempted to prevent him from entering. Bass inflicted terrible injuries on Mrs. Sloan, and then ran into the room and murdered his wife. Mrs. Sloan was removed to the Infirmary, but succumbed to the injuries.

Bass disappeared, and a reward of £100 was offered for his apprehension. No fewer than forty persons were arrested on suspicion of being the wanted man, both in Scotland and England, so that the "tramps" must have had a bad time. Bass was at length captured near Ellon, on the 12th March, while asking help from a farmer.

Mr. Wallace, for the defence, said that no case since the M'Lachlan trial had stirred public feeling to such an extent as this one, and moved that the proceedings should take place at Edinburgh to secure an impartial investigation. The Lord Justice-Clerk, after consulting with his colleague, Lord Young, said the trial must proceed. A special defence of insanity was put forward. Evidence was led. The jury found both charges proved, and also added that they were of the opinion the prisoner was of sound mind on the day in question. Sentence of death was passed, to be carried out within the South Prison of Glasgow, on the 31st May. Bass, after sentence was passed, delivered an address in a hysterical manner. Holding up his hand, he took an oath that he was innocent. There was no public sympathy extended to the condemned man, and he duly paid the penalty.

1878.

May 8—11. Before the High Court of Justiciary at Edinburgh, the Lord Justice-Clerk on the Bench. Eugene Marie Chantrelle (44), a French teacher in the city, was charged with the murder of his wife, by administering opium in certain articles of food, in January, within his house, 81A George Street, Edinburgh.

The Lord Advocate Watson (afterwards Lord Watson of Thankerton), and the Solicitor-General, Macdonald (afterwards Lord Justice-Clerk), conducted the case for the Crown, while for the defence the counsel were all men of marked ability who afterwards adorned the Bench—Mr. Trayner, Mr. J. P. B. Robertson, and Mr. Thomas Shaw (the late Lord Craigmyle*).

Chantrelle was a native of Nantes, and came to Edinburgh as a teacher in Newington Academy. He unfortunately formed an intimacy with one of his pupils, Elizabeth Cullen Dyer, who was about sixteen years of age. In order to hide his shame he married her. The first of the four children was born two months after the marriage in August, 1868. Their married life was unhappy, and the young wife had to seek shelter for some time with her mother when his treatment became unbearable. He had threatened her with a pistol, and also said he would poison her.

On account of his immoral habits his classes became deserted, which resulted in debt. In 1877, Chantrelle had effected an insurance policy over his wife's life for £1,000, which included "accidental death." He was careful to make inquiries what was the exact meaning of the term before taking out the policy.

The principal witness for the Crown was Mary Byrne, the servant. She deponed that on New Year Day of 1878 she was given a holiday. In the evening when she returned home, her mistress was unwell in bed. Next morning madame was worse and moaning in great pain. There was a strong smell of gas perceptible in the room. Dr. Carmichael was sent for. When the doctor arrived, thinking the symptoms were somewhat unusual he called in Dr. Littlejohn, the police surgeon (afterwards Sir Henry). They ordered the removal of madame to the Royal Infirmary, where she died in the course of the afternoon. The doctors were of opinion that death was due to narcotic poisoning, but a *post mortem*, curiously, failed to corroborate their suspicions. This was, however, accounted for by certain stains of vomit found on the deceased's night-dress and on the bed clothes, which had been subjected to analysis, and confirmed the suspicion that the deceased had died from opium. The Crown alleged Chantrelle had broken the gas pipe in order to divert suspicion.

---

* See " The Other Bundle," by the late Lord Craigmyle.

Other witnesses, including Mrs. Dyer, mother of the deceased, testified to the bad treatment her daughter had received from Chantrelle, even from the time of their marriage. A number of medical men and chemists were examined for the defence. They generally were of the opinion that it was impossible to distinguish between gas and opium poisoning. This was all the evidence Mr. Trayner could bring forth, and when he closed his case, Chantrelle, who throughout the trial had remained quiet, inquired: " Is this all the evidence for the defence? " The jury took an hour to consider their verdict, which was a unanimous one of guilty.

After sentence of death was passed, Chantrelle, who seemed rather surprised at the decision of the jury, asked the judge if he could make some remarks. Waving his hand excitedly and speaking in broken English, he gave a long harangue about the presence of the stain of opium, which, he alleged, had been rubbed in by some other person. In the end, his Lordship had to intervene, and said that the prisoner should not proceed further, and if there was anything else to say it should be through his agent. Chantrelle then resumed his seat, and the Court slowly cleared. A reprieve was refused, and the unfortunate man paid the penalty in the Calton Jail, on Friday, the 31st Mây. Marwood was the hangman.

Chantrelle was quite indifferent to religious matters. When confined in prison he was first visited by a Roman Catholic priest, and then by the Rev. George Wilson, of the Tolbooth Church. Like Pritchard, he was hanged in the mourning clothes he wore at the funeral of his wife. Before the procession was formed to the scaffold, Mr. Wilson inquired if he had any confession to make. In a clear, ringing voice, Chantrelle replied: " I have nothing to confess, Mr. Wilson." He was the only man of education in Scotland for many years to tread the scaffold, with the exception of Pritchard, his rival in crime. He held the degree of B.A., and was the author of several school text books, including " Reading Lessons in Latin."

[We have been informed that his eldest son for many years carried on a tobacconist's business under an assumed name in Edinburgh. Chantrelle's wife was buried in the Dyer's ground in the Grange Cemetery, but her name has not been included on the stone, the lettering of which is now getting indistinct. The grave is situated at the South Walk, a little to the right of the road which comes under the terrace. It is somewhat remarkable that the Grange Cemetery contains the remains of two murderers' victims, both having died from the effects of poison.]

September 6 and 7. At Perth Circuit Court, before Lord Mure, William M'Donald, a fisherman, from St. Andrews, was charged with the murder of his wife by shooting her with a gun, on the 13th June. M'Donald then attempted to take his own life. Evidence was led at considerable length. The jury, by a majority, found the prisoner guilty, but strongly recommended him to mercy. On inquiry by his Lordship, the foreman intimated the majorities 13 to 2 and 11 to 4 respectively. Sentence of death was passed, to be carried out within the walls of Cupar Prison, on the 3rd October. Strong efforts were made to secure a commutation of the sentence, but Mr. Cross, the Home Secretary, decided the law must take its course.

The execution created much interest in the County town. The scaffold was erected in the garden at the south side of the prison, and could be seen from the hills a mile away. The drop was brought over a ventilator ten or twelve feet high. M'Donald met his fate with stolid indifference. He alleged that he was innocent of the murder, and it was committed by mutual agreement to put an end to the misery in which they had been living. A large crowd assembled around the prison to witness the hoisting of the black flag. Marwood was the hangman. M'Donald's remains were subsequently buried in front of the east door of the jail, but there is no mark to indicate the grave.

[Mr. Donaldson was the governor. He was much respected, and continued in charge until the prison ceased to be used as a place of detention in 1885. The old jail is now utilised as a dwelling-house by a market gardener. Twenty-five years had passed since there had been an execution in Cupar—the brothers Scanlan—for murder.

" A. K. H. B.," in one of his books, recalls the case of M'Donald. He says: "The prisoner shot his wife dead, then shot himself and seemed dying. I forthwith saw the poor wretch, and prayed with him earnestly hoping he would die, but the doctors nursed him back to life again, and he was hanged. Had I been a doctor, I would have let him slip away. . . . He was mad. His father had committed suicide before him. . . . I always had a moral disapproval of the Home Secretary, who hanged him in the face of a petition signed by all St. Andrews."]

September 15. At Inverness Circuit Court, before Lord Deas, Isaac Williamson, a hawker, was charged with the murder of his wife, on the road between Inverness and Fort Augustus. Lord Deas, in summing up, said that he could not see one single circumstance in the evidence that would justify them bringing in any other verdict short of murder. If there had been such a circumstance he would have been glad to point it out. A verdict of culpable homicide was, however, returned. Remarking that the jury had taken a merciful view, Lord Deas passed sentence of penal servitude for life.

1881.

December 27 and 28. At Glasgow Circuit Court, before Lord Deas—(Old Court)—Thomas Ferguson was found guilty of the murder of his wife, in a house in John Knox Street, Glasgow. A plea of insanity had been put forward by the defence. The jury coupled the verdict with a recommendation to mercy on account of weak mind.

Lord Deas, in passing sentence, said what might be the effects of the recommendation of the jury to the Crown was not for him to say, but it would not be consistent with his duty to say any more to the Crown than he had done to the jury. Although he had no doubt they gave every attention to their duty, they did not consider they could return the verdict in the form he had suggested. The Crown would be aware of the fact that he had suggested a more lenient verdict to the jury, but over and above that it would not be his province nor his duty to say any more in that respect. He would strongly recommend the prisoner not to put any trust in the hope that the recommendation of the jury would receive effect. Ferguson exclaimed, after sentence was passed: "I know I am guilty, but I was not myself when I did it."

[This is perhaps one of the very few instances when a verdict of culpable homicide was put forward by Lord Deas but was not acted upon by the jury. In numerous other similar cases it was the other way about, as in the trial of Williamson in 1878. His Lordship was a terror to evil doers, and was sometimes termed "Lord Death" or the "hanging judge." It was said that he once declared at Glasgow that he would clear the city of its thieves by his exemplary sentences of fifteen or twenty years' penal servitude, so that he could hang up his watch and chain to a lamp post, go for a walk, and on coming back find them both intact.]

1882.

October 24. Before the High Court of Justiciary at Edinburgh, Lord Craighill on the Bench, Charles Soutar, a rat-catcher, from Aberdeen, was charged with violating the tomb of the Earl of Crawford and Balcarres, at Dunecht. The circumstances were most peculiar and almost unexampled in the mysteries of crime.

The 25th Earl of Crawford and the 8th Earl of Balcarres died at Florence, in December, 1880. Encased in three coffins, one of which was lead, the body was brought home to Dunecht. A violent snowstorm occurred, and the hearse was snowed up for some days before it returned to Aberdeen. The body was laid in the mausoleum, access to which was gained by raising a stone slab outside the chapel and descending a flight of stairs. It took no fewer than eight men to place the coffins, which weighed about ten cwts., on the niche. The vault was then closed.

Time passed, and in the following June a workman passing the entrance felt a peculiar smell emanating from the vault. It was thought that it might come from decayed flowers. No one suspected that a gross outrage had taken place. An anonymous letter received in September by the Commissioner for Lord Crawford stated the remains were not in the vault as it was supposed. It seemed to have been expected by the conspirators that the Dowager Lady Crawford would herself have visited the vault and made the discovery. One trembles to think what would have happened had she done so. The desecration had, therefore, to be announced by an anonymous letter. This, however, had not the desired effect, as the Commissioner believed that it was only a hoax.

Two months elapsed, when one morning in December it was found that the slab had been raised and the railings surrounding the entrance pulled down. The police were now informed, and on descending the stair they discovered the coffins had been forced open and the body taken away. The floor was strewn with coffins and their lids, while the leaden shell had been cut open. A similar odour to that which the workman smelled in June came from the sawdust in which the body was packed, and not from the decayed flowers as it had been thought. There was now no question that the body had been removed in June. A careful search of the grounds was made, and even a bloodhound employed, but still there was no trace of the remains.

As it was believed the body had been stolen for the sake of ransom, the Government did not at first offer a reward, but later the sum of £600 was offered to anyone who could give such information as would lead to the conviction of the perpetrators. The body was subsequently discovered in the grounds, lying in a ditch, covered over with leaves and rolled in a blanket. Several arrests followed, but only Soutar was put on trial.

The Solicitor-General (Asher) conducted the prosecution, while the Dean of Faculty, Mr. Macdonald (afterwards the Lord Justice-Clerk) and Mr. Mackenzie (afterwards Lord Mackenzie) were the principal counsel for the defence.

Soutar, in his declaration, told a remarkable story. He said one night when poaching in a wood near Dunecht House, he came upon four men carrying a body, who bound him over, under pain of death, not to reveal what he had seen. Among the witnesses for the Crown was George Machray, a gamekeeper, who spoke to a conversation he had with Soutar over the case. It was not disputed by the Crown that there must have been others concerned in the outrage, and the Dean commented upon this in his address to the jury. Soutar was found guilty, and sentenced to five years' penal servitude.

[The case bristled with difficulties, and there can be little doubt the mystery was only partially cleared up, as the Crown admitted. Two motives might be put forward for the outrage— one to wreak vengeance on the family, the other for the purpose of securing a ransom. A year or two ago the writer visited

Dunecht, one of the most palatial mansions in Scotland, and even after half-a-century the famous case is still fresh in the recollection of old residenters.

In the vaults below Parliament House, Edinburgh, a veritable chamber of horrors, are the "productions" in all the trials— knives, pistols, etc., but in addition there is a massive shell of a coffin, which bears the words:—

Alexander William Crawford Lindsay,
25th Earl of Crawford and 8th Earl of Balcarres.
Born 16th October, 1812.   Died 13th December, 1880.

Considerable difficulty was experienced in allocating the reward, and Sheriff Guthrie Smith adjudicated in favour of Machray, but did not award the full amount.]

1883.

April 25.   At Glasgow Circuit Court, before Lord Deas—(Old Court)—Henry Mullen and Martin Scott were charged with the murder of two gamekeepers on the farm of Devol, near Port-Glasgow, in February.   Mr. R. Vary Campbell, Advocate-Depute, prosecuted, while Dean of Faculty Macdonald conducted the defence.   The tragedy was discovered by the wife of a farmer, who was returning by a short cut across the fields in the evening. The men, who were dead, had received terrible injuries with a gun, which had been fired at such close quarters that the shot had blackened their faces.

A number of well-known poachers were arrested, but all were liberated except the two prisoners and another, named Kyle, who turned informer.   Lord Deas summed up at great length, in the course of which he indicated that it would be dangerous to convict one and not the other.   His Lordship said that he could not advise that there was any ground for a verdict short of murder.   The jury unanimously found the men guilty.   Lord Deas, in an impressive address, passed sentence of death, to be carried out within Duke Street Prison, Glasgow, on the 17th May.   Strong efforts were made to secure a reprieve, all the jurors signing the petition, but it was refused.

On account of Marwood's absence in Ireland in connection with the Phœnix Park murderers, the execution was delayed until the 23rd May. This was the first execution carried out in Duke Street Prison.

September 10. At Jedburgh Circuit Court, a trial for child murder had to be abandoned on account of the jurymen having been countermanded by the Depute-Clerk.

[There is no record of such an occurrence previously, and probably such an unfortunate incident will never take place again.]

1883.

December 17 to 21. Before the High Court of Justiciary at Edinburgh, the Lord Justice-Clerk and Lords Mure and Craighill on the bench. The trial proceeded of what was known as the Glasgow Dynamiters—ten men—M'Dermott, Devaney, Calligan, M'Cann, M'Culloch, Donnelly, Kelly, M'Cabe, Drum, and Casey. They were all charged with having, on the 20th January, blown up a gasometer at Tradestown, Glasgow, containing 3,500 cubic feet of gas. Another charge was also libelled for having attempted to blow up the Canal Bridge at Possil Park, Glasgow.

The Lord Advocate, Mr. J. B. Balfour (afterwards Lord Kinross), prosecuted, assisted by Mr. Brand and Mr. Æneas J. G. Mackay, Advocate-Depute. Among the counsel for the defence were Mr. C. J. Guthrie (Lord Guthrie), Mr. J. F. M'Lennan (Sheriff M'Lennan), Mr. N. J. D. Kennedy (Lord Kennedy), and Mr. R. L. Orr (Sheriff Orr), the last-named being the only surviving Advocate who took part in the trial. There were 158 Crown witnesses, while the "productions" numbered 128, and included dynamite, revolvers, and threatening letters sent to the Lord Provost of Glasgow and the Chief Constable.

A plea of not guilty was tendered, while a special defence of alibi was intimated. It was averred that the men belonged to a brotherhood known as the "Irish Physical Force Society," a Fenian organisation whose aim was to overawe the Government. Had the canal aqueduct been blown up it was believed thousands in the lower quarters of the city would have been drowned.

The arrest of the men was mainly brought about by a constable named Porter, whose beat was at the entrance to Glasgow Green. For some time he had observed a number of men who met daily near the Nelson Monument. They appeared to be in deep conversation and frequently examined papers. What roused the suspicion of the constable was that whenever he passed the conversation ceased. Their movements were so suspicious that he watched from a distance by means of a telescope. An informer, named George Hughes was an important witness for the Crown. The defence alleged that the explosion might have been the work of a prominent Fenian leader named Featherstone, who was in Glasgow on the 20th January. He had been sentenced at Liverpool in August, along with three other men, to penal servitude for life for a Fenian crime. Another fact which was put forward by the defence was that four other members of the Society who were in Glasgow on the dates mentioned in the indictment had already been sentenced in London.

The jury found all the men guilty. Five were convicted of treason—felony, and the remainder guilty of conspiracy. Sentence of penal servitude for life was passed on the five, while the remainder were sentenced to seven years' penal servitude.

[The trial created much general interest and also considerable alarm. It had been freely rumoured that an attempt would be made by their companions to effect a rescue even from their places in the dock. A detachment of Gordon Highlanders was therefore stationed in Parliament Square, while the police in the vicinity of the Court were provided with revolvers.

The men were brought through from Glasgow under an armed escort, and were confined during the trial in the cells under the High Court. As a whole the men were a miserable and dejected looking lot, and seemed hardly capable of "overawing the Laws of the Realm," according to the wording of the indictment.

Sir J. H. A. Macdonald, in his "Jottings," recounts a few amusing episodes about the men's arrival in Edinburgh. He was then a prison commissioner, and asked them in the cells if they wished to say anything. The eldest replied with a fine Irish brogue, "Indade, sor, oi think we ought to have some refreshment."

In order to ensure the safety of the Crown witnesses from

H

Glasgow the entire railway route was guarded by police. A stalwart constable, baton in hand, sat behind each prisoner in the dock, which was enlarged for the occasion. Although the trial passed off without any serious incident, either with a view to interfering with the. witnesses or the prisoners, the authorities believed the unusual precautions more than justified. After the trial the men were detained for a few days in the Calton Jail. Great secrecy was observed regarding their removal to Chatham Prison. They were taken down to St. Margaret's Station in a prison van. Another had left the prison some minutes earlier and proceeded along Princes Street to draw the crowd away. The men were taken south in a travelling prison van which was brought up from St. Margaret's to the Waverley and attached to the forenoon London train. Captain Christie, Governor of the Calton Prison, and an armed escort, accompanied the prisoners.

It need not be said that there was a feeling of relief to all concerned when Edinburgh saw the last of the Dynamiters. The tension and alarm of their ten days' stay in the capital was one to be remembered. The last of the "life" men were liberated in 1901, and the obligation to report to the police was cancelled in 1905.]

1884.

March 10. Before the High Court of Justiciary at Edinburgh, Lord Young on the bench. Robert Flockart Vickars and William Innes, miners, residing at Gorebridge, were charged with the murder of two assistant gamekeepers, named John Fortune and John M'Diarmid. They were also charged with seriously assaulting James Grosset, head gamekeeper, at Rosebery.

The gamekeepers, who were employed on Lord Rosebery's estate, which is situated at the foot of Moorfoot Hills, had gone out to look for poachers. It was a clear frosty morning on the 15th December, while overhead the moon was full. About 3 a.m., the gamekeepers came upon the men, who were armed with guns. On being called to surrender, one of the poachers said to the other, " Take that on the left and I will do for that on the right." A moment later the guns were discharged and the two watchers fell fatally injured. Before the firearms could be reloaded, Grosset made off with the following words ringing in his ear, "Quick, don't let him away; we'll catch him at the bridge" (meaning the bridge which spans the South Esk), shouted by one of the men to the other. However, by changing his course Grosset arrived safely at Edgelaw Farm, and awakened Mr. Simpson, the farmer, who drove into Gorebridge and informed Sergeant Adamson. Fortune and M'Diarmid were at once removed to the Edinburgh Royal Infirmary, but they succumbed to their injuries, Fortune on the 18th December and M'Diarmid on the 8th January. Grosset was able to furnish such information as led to the arrest of the men, both noted poachers.

The Solicitor-General (Asher) conducted the prosecution, while the Dean of Faculty (Macdonald) appeared for the prisoners. The defence was a complete denial that the men had ever left their own houses at Gorebridge at the time libelled. After an absence of forty-nine minutes the jury, at 7.50 p.m., found the charges proved. Lord Young, who expressed his complete concurrence with the verdict, passed sentence of death, to be carried out in the Calton Jail, Edinburgh, on the 31st March. A week after conviction the men admitted shooting the gamekeepers.

Efforts to obtain a reprieve proved unsuccessful. Both men, particularly Vickars, thought that mercy would be extended to them. Even when he took his place on the drop he was buoyed up with the hope that a last minute reprieve would arrive. A dense crowd assembled outside the prison and on the Calton Hill. Waterloo Place was blocked with a seething mass of people to witness the hoisting of the signal at eight o'clock. Considerable speculation arose as minute after minute passed, but at length, at twelve minutes past the hour, the black flag run up on the prison flagstaff to half-mast proclaimed to all who beheld it that the Gorebridge poachers had gone to their doom. The execution was carried out by James Berry and an assistant, Richard Chester.

[In a somewhat rare volume, entitled "Experiences of an Executioner," Berry gives minute details of the final scene and his four days' stay in the Calton Jail. This was the first execution he carried through.]

1889.

February 5. At Inverness Circuit Court, before the Lord Justice-Clerk (Lord Kingsburgh*), Hector M'Donald was found guilty of the murder of a widow, named Lamont, at Fort George. Sentence of death was passed, to be carried out at Inverness on the 4th March. A man in the gallery gave a horrid shriek and fainted when sentence was pronounced. Sentence commuted.

[Fifty years had passed since a capital conviction had been returned at Inverness. The prison was then situated adjoining the Courthouse on the prominent Castle Buildings, which are such an imposing feature of the town.]

February 18. Before the High Court of Justiciary at Edinburgh, the Lord Justice-Clerk on the bench, Jessie King was convicted of two charges of murder—young children committed to her charge. She resided in the Stockbridge district of the city. Another count in the indictment was found not proven. Jessie King was a " baby farmer " of the worst and most depraved type. Although she was found guilty of the murder of only two children it was believed that she was responsible for the death of several others. She frequently changed from one quarter of the city to another, and assumed various names to put the police off her track.

A man name Pearson, who was her paramour, gave testimony for the Crown. There was no evidence led for the defence. His Lordship, in summing up, said the acts were deliberate and intentional, and not committed in a frenzy of passion. There was no case that he had ever heard of or read of in which such facts as had been disclosed where a verdict of culpable homicide had been returned. The jury were absent forty minutes in considering their verdict. A painful scene followed when sentence was passed. The unfortunate woman groaned and shrieked in the most heart-rending manner and finally collapsed in a fainting fit. She was carried from the dock by two policemen to the cells below. The sentence was fixed to be carried out in the Calton Jail on the 11th March.

During her incarceration she twice attempted suicide. One afternoon a wardress discovered she had a long pin in her

---

*Mr. J. H. A. Macdonald, Dean of Faculty, appointed August, 1888.

possession. When challenged, Jessie explained it was for picking her teeth. How she came into possession of it could never be explained, but it was certain that she had other designs with the pin than she had said. On another occasion a piece of hemp rope was found in her cell.

Several petitions were forwarded to the Home Secretary on her behalf. She was from the first in the belief that the capital sentence would not be carried out. When informed by the two junior Magistrates that the law must take its course she was totally overcome. Canon Donlevey was most assiduous in his ministrations and attended her to the last, chanting a litany on the short walk to the scaffold. Jessie King, with a calm fortitude which was astonishing, thanked the officials for their kindness to her. When she was leaving the cell a group of wardresses in tears were waiting to say good-bye. Berry was the executioner.

[Jessie King was born in the Anderston district of Glasgow in 1861, and worked at the mills there for some time. She, however, migrated to Edinburgh, and was employed as a laundry worker at Causewayside. She was the only woman who had paid the last penalty in Scotland since 1853.]

March 25. At Dundee Circuit Court, before Lord Young, William Henry Bury was charged with the murder of his wife, in a house in Princes Street, Dundee, on the 3rd February. The evidence led was sensational. According to the police witnesses, Bury had rushed into the police office on a Sunday evening, and exclaimed: "I'm Jack the Ripper; if you go to my house you will find the body of my wife, which I have cut up and placed in a box." The confession was at first ridiculed, but on further assurance the man was detained. The police, proceeding to the house, found the statement was correct. The body, which was found in a large packing case, was in a horribly mutilated condition.

The jury retired at 9.55 p.m., and after an absence of twenty-five minutes returned with a verdict of guilty with a recommendation to mercy. Lord Young inquired on what ground was the recommendation. A juryman: "Partly because of the conflicting medical evidence." Lord Young replied that "there was no ground for the recommendation under that head, and the jury must retire again to consider the verdict, because it left a doubt as to the prisoner's guilt." After an absence of five minutes the jury returned with a "unanimous verdict of guilty." Sentence of death was passed, to take effect within Dundee Prison on the 24th April. The Court rose, having sat almost continuously for thirteen hours.

Bury made a detailed confession, and forwarded to the Home Secretary a document which was said made some startling revelations on the Whitechapel murders in London, but the statement was never made public. Bury duly paid the penalty. Berry was the executioner.

[In connection with the confession forwarded to the Home Secretary, it is a fact that the atrocious tragedies in London ceased about a week after Bury's arrival in Dundee from the metropolis. He was well known in the east end of London, and several of his landlords gave him a bad character, while blood stains were found in his rooms. To the public, at least, mystery still surrounds the Whitechapel murders to this day.

A stone in the courtyard of the Old Jail, now the police garage, with the lettering and date, "W.H.B. 24/4/1889," is a grim reminder of the famous case. Forty-two years had passed since the last execution in Dundee.]

November 4. Before the High Court of Justiciary at Edinburgh, the Lord Justice-Clerk on the bench, John Watson Laurie, described as "lately a prisoner in the prison of Greenock," was charged with the murder of Edwin Robert Rose, at Glen Sannox, Arran, on the 15th July. Mr. Moir, Solicitor-General (afterwards Lord Stormonth-Darling), prosecuted, with Mr. A. Graham Murray (now Lord Dunedin) and Mr. Dugald M'Kechnie. The defence was in the hands of Mr. J. B. Balfour, Dean of Faculty (afterwards Lord Kinross) and Mr. Scott Dickson (afterwards Lord Scott Dickson).

Remarkable evidence was led for the prosecution. It appeared that Laurie, who was a pattern-maker in Glasgow, was masquerading under the name of "Mr. Annandale" at Rothesay during the Fair week in July. He struck up an acquaintance during a sail from Rothesay to Arran on board the "Ivanhoe," a famous boat of its day on the Clyde, with a London clerk named Edwin Robert Rose, who was also on holiday. The upshot of this acquaintance was that they both agreed to return to Arran in a couple of days to spend the week-end, and climb Goatfell together. For this purpose they engaged a room at Invercloy, Brodick, and returned again to Rothesay.

They duly set out for Arran as arranged on the 13th July. In the interval Rose had introduced his friend, " Mr. Annandale," to two tourists who were also going to Arran for the week-end. It so happened that one of the tourists did not like the personality of " Mr. Annandale," and warned Rose, who was a man with plenty of money and evidently in a totally different walk of life, to have nothing more to do with him. Rose, however, did not act upon this advice, and on Monday both climbed Goatfell together. " Mr. Annandale " returned to his lodgings alone in the evening, and told his landlady that his friend had been suddenly called back to London.

The relations of Rose, who became alarmed at his non-appearance at the close of his holiday, instituted inquiries. It was pretty well established by the police that he had not left the island. Numerous search-parties scoured Goatfell and the surrounding district for the missing man, who veritably seemed to have vanished into space. After some time his mangled remains were found lying under a large boulder at the foot of a precipice on Goatfell. The pockets were empty, while under a stone several articles, including a stick and a cap which belonged to Rose, were discovered.

" Mr. Annandale " or Laurie, who had meantime returned to Rothesay, and had been seen wearing some of the dead man's clothes, now disappeared. A warrant was issued for his apprehension on the charge of murder. This elusive pattern-maker took the unusual course of replying to the charge made against him by writing letters to the " N.B. Daily Mail " and the " Glasgow Herald." For the next week or two he was reported as being in various places at the same time, but was at length run to earth, on the 3rd September, near Larkhall, after an exciting chase. He attempted to commit suicide—when hotly pursued—by cutting his throat with a razor.

The Crown alleged that the prisoner had thrown Rose over a cliff, beaten him to death, and then buried the body under a heap of stones. For the defence it was maintained that the injuries could easily have been accounted for by a fall. The jury, after an absence of forty minutes, returned to Court at 9.45 p.m., with a verdict of guilty by a majority. The Lord Justice-Clerk passed sentence of death, to be carried out within Greenock Prison on the 30th November. Laurie turned round, and looking up to the gallery, said in a clear voice: "Ladies and gentlemen, I am innocent of the charge." He was attempting to proceed further when his Lordship said the prisoner would not be allowed to make a speech, and Laurie was then removed.

Petitions for a reprieve were at once set on foot, stating that the prisoner was not fully responsible for his actions and that there had been insanity in the family. The appeal for signatures met with much success, particularly in the west of Scotland, where Laurie had many relatives in comfortable circumstances. In consequence of the petitions, Lord Lothian, the Home Secretary, ordered that Laurie should be examined as to his soundness of mind by several medical experts. Two days before the date appointed for the execution, the Home Secretary intimated that the capital sentence was commuted to penal servitude for life in view of the medical report. All the arrangements for the execution were practically complete when the news of the respite was conveyed to the Magistrates of Greenock.

[Laurie thus instead of concluding his earthly existence by the hands of Berry was removed to Peterhead to serve his sentence. A few years later he attempted to escape, but was soon captured. Latterly his mind gave way and he was confined in the Lunatic Department of Perth Penitentiary, where he died on the 4th October, 1930, almost forty-one years since the date of the trial.]

1890.

August 11. At Ayr Circuit Court, before the Lord Justice-Clerk,* John M'Donald was found guilty of the murder of his wife and a lodger, named Wauch, at Linkieburn, Muirkirk, in June.

---

* It seldom happens that a judge sentences a man to death bearing his own name but not the full initials.

The defence, which was conducted by Mr. Crabb Watt, was to the effect that on the date libelled the prisoner was insane. The verdict of the jury was returned by a majority of nine to six, coupled with a unanimous recommendation to mercy because there was a want of motive and because the murder was not premeditated. Sentence of death was pronounced, to be carried out within Ayr Prison on the 1st September. Sentence commuted.

September 2. At Glasgow Circuit Court, before Lord Adam (Old Court), Henry Delven (45), a miner, was found guilty of the murder of his wife at Benhar, near Shotts, in June. The jury accompanied the verdict with a unanimous recommendation to mercy.

Delven, who left a family of seven, was hanged within Duke Street Prison, Glasgow, on the 23rd September. When the black flag was hoisted a man in the crowd fainted.

September 3. At Glasgow Circuit Court, before Lord Adam (Old Court), Thomas Gribbins, an old man, was convicted of murder by stabbing in the Saltmarket, in July. The verdict was coupled with a unanimous recommendation to mercy. Sentence commuted.

December 29. At Glasgow Circuit Court, before Lord Stormonth-Darling (Old Court), Loreto Palambo, an Italian, was found guilty of the murder of ·a fellow-countryman in Possil Road, Glasgow, in November. The jury added a recommendation to mercy. Sentence commuted.

[It is said that his sweetheart acted the part of a modern "Jeanie Deans." She walked all the way to London and personally pleaded with Lord Lothian, the Home Secrettary, that mercy should be extended to her lover. In this she was successful. Palambo was subsequently liberated on licence after serving ten years of his life sentence, and proceeded back to his native country. History unfortunately is silent about the love romance.]

1891.

December 21. At Glasgow Circuit Court, before Lord Adam (Old Court), Frederick Thomas Storey (54), a circus manager, employed at Cooke's Circus, Greenock, was found guilty of the murder of Lizzie Pastor, also employed at the circus, by stabbing her, in Argyle Street, Greenock, on the 14th March. Storey had manifested great affection for her, but it was not reciprocated, and he murdered her out of revenge. Storey was hanged on the 11th January, within Greenock Prison.

[This prison, which was situated behind the County Buildings in Nelson Street, has now been taken down. A new one was erected some years ago at Gateside, on the western outskirts of the town.]

1892.

May 9. At Glasgow Circuit Court, before the Lord Justice-Clerk (Old Court), Alexander Robertson was found guilty of the murder of a woman at Keppochhill, Glasgow. The jury coupled the verdict with a recommendation to mercy. Sentence commuted.

[This was the last capital case before Lord Kingsburgh (Sir J. H. A. Macdonald). Although during the next twenty years many serious homicide charges passed through his hands, in none was the capital verdict returned. His Lordship had strong religious convictions, and was not ashamed to be found on his knees in prayer when a jury had retired in a capital case. He never made any social engagement when a person who had come before him was under sentence of death.

Lord Kinnear, who abhorred murder charges, occasionally invoked the assistance of Lord Kingsburgh to take a murder trial at Glasgow, after the other business of the Court had been conducted, but in none of those instances was the verdict murder.]

December 27 and 28. At Glasgow Circuit Court, before Lord Adam (Old Court), William M'Keown, along with a seaman, was charged with the murder of a woman in a house at Pollockshields, Glasgow, in October. M'Keown, a gardener, had been left in charge of his employer's house in Maxwell Drive. When the woman failed to turn up, inquiries were made as to what had become of her. It was known that she had been near the house, and the police, after making investigation, found the remains of the woman buried in the garden, the body having been horribly mutilated. M'Keown absconded, but was arrested near Cardonald with his throat cut in an attempt to commit suicide.

M'Keown pleaded guilty to culpable homicide, but this was not accepted by the Crown, while the seaman pleaded alibi. A request for separate trials was refused. Evidence was then led, during part of which the alibi was established and the man was discharged. The defence alleged that the woman had been cut after she was dead, but this fact had not been mentioned in the panel's declaration, which no doubt influenced the jury. A unanimous verdict of guilty was returned, and he was sentenced to death. Efforts to obtain a reprieve proved unavailing, and M'Keown paid the full penalty within Duke Street Prison, Glasgow, on the 18th January.

December 28. At Glasgow Circuit Court, before Lord Stormonth-Darling (New Court), David Forrester was found guilty of wife murder at Stenhousemuir, in October. Insanity was put forward by the defence, but a unanimous verdict of guilty, accompanied by a strong recommendation to mercy, was returned. Sentence commuted.

[This is the only instance of two capital sentences having been pronounced in Glasgow in both Courts in one day, with the exception of a similar instance in 1904. Several hours elapsed between them in 1892, but in 1904 they were almost simultaneous.]

1893.

July 1. At Aberdeen Circuit Court, before Lord M'Laren, Robert Smith, a farm employé, was found guilty of culpable homicide, causing the death of a fellow workman and fatally injuring another, on a farm near Stonehaven. The case was described by his Lordship as upon the very edge of murder, and sentence of penal servitude for life was passed.

[It has been said that once, when his old employer went to see him at Peterhead, the fact was mentioned that a petition might be set on foot to the Home Secretary to mitigate the sentence. Smith exclaimed: "Dae nae such thing. I was never so happy and comfortable all my life. The meat is guid and aye sure, and ye ha'e a roof abune your heid. It's far better than

howin' neeps or howkin' tatties." Peterhead convict establish-
ment does not get praise like that every day.]

December 12 to 22. Tuesday to Friday. Before the High
Court of Justiciary at Edinburgh, the Lord Justice-Clerk on the
bench, there commenced one of the most remarkable and com-
plicated trials in Scotland since that of Jessie M'Lachlan in 1862.
This was the Ardlamont case.

Alfred John Monson (32), shooting tenant of Ardlamont, Argyll,
and Edward Sweeney, alias Davis, alias Scott, were charged with
attempt to murder Windsor Dudley Cecil Hambrough, by boring
or causing a hole to be bored in a rowing boat, and having plugged
the hole did remove it in Ardlamont Bay, whereby the boat was
swamped on the night of 9th-10th August, and the said Windsor
Dudley Cecil Hambrough was thrown into the sea. In addition
there was a charge of murder. The Crown alleged that, on the
10th August, Monson and Scott did shoot Hambrough in a wood
some 360 yards from the mansion house. A galaxy of talent
appeared for the Crown and the defence.

Mr. Asher, Solicitor-General, represented the prosecution,
assisted by Messrs. Strachan, Reid, and Lorimer, Advocates-
Depute. Mr. Comrie Thomson, for the defence, had the assistance
of Messrs. John Wilson and William Findlay. Curiously, only
one of the foregoing members of the bar ever reached the more
serene atmosphere of the bench. This was Mr. John Wilson
(the late Lord Ashmore). Mr. R. C. Malcolm, Advocate (now
Sheriff Malcolm of Dundee), watched the case on behalf of Major
Hambrough.

The diet having been called against Monson and Scott, Monson
pleaded not guilty, but Scott was not present, or according to the
wording of the indictment: "Being conscious of your guilt in
the premises did abscond and flee from justice." After the
formality of having Scott's name called by the Macer in
Parliament Hall, on the motion of the Solicitor-General, his
Lordship passed sentence of outlawry.

As a preliminary to the trial some facts about Monson and
his associates may be here not inopportune. Monson, who was
of good family, had a somewhat varied career. He had married

at the Cape, and on coming home tried to eke out a livelihood as an Army tutor. Through a friend of his, Mr. Tottenham, a financial agent in London, he made the acquaintance of Major Hambrough, who owned large estates in the south of England. Like Monson, the Major was in need of money, as his life interest in the estates had been mortgaged. Mr. Tottenham came to his assistance and made an advance. It had been arranged that the Major's son, Cecil, should follow his father's footsteps and go into the Army. Monson was to be his tutor, and was to receive a salary of £300 for board and tutelage. After staying at various places in England, Monson, his wife and family, along with Hambrough, took up residence at Riseley Hall, Yorkshire, where they remained a year. He was financed by his friend, Mr. Tottenham, but in the end Monson became bankrupt, and had to leave the district.

Hambrough, who was heir of entail to his father's estates on attaining his majority in about a year's time, could have sold his life interest for a large sum. Monson now, for some reason difficult to explain, was negotiating to buy Ardlamont Estate for Hambrough, but the sum wanted by the agents was too high. However, in May, 1893, he had entered into a lease of the house and shootings, purporting to be for Hambrough, at a rent of £450. As Monson was still an undischarged bankrupt and Hambrough under age, the name of a Mr. Jerningham, of Staines, Middlesex, appeared on the lease. Monson had represented to the Ardlamont agents in Edinburgh that Mr. Jerningham was Hambrough's guardian and a man of means, while the lad himself woould come into money when he reached his majority.

Monson was no sooner settled at Ardlamont than he made several attempts to effect an insurance on the life of Hambrough for £50,000, but was unsuccessful. In the end, by false statements, he succeeded in insuring the young man's life with the Mutual Life Insurance Company of New York in two policies of £10,000 each. This was on the 4th August. They were assigned to Mrs. Monson, and the first premium of £194 was paid by Monson from money he had received from Mr. Tottenham which he had represented he wished for another purpose.

Hambrough, who was entirely under the influence of Monson,

wrote out a remarkable letter to Mrs. Monson in those terms: "If you will pay the premiums on the two policies of my life of £10,000 each with the Mutual Life Insurance Company of New York, I am willing that you should hold the policies as security for all monies due to you from me, and as security against all liabilities incurred by you on my behalf, and in the event of my death occurring before the repayment of these monies you will be the sole beneficiary of these policies, and I have given notice to the Mutual Life Insurance Company of New York that you are the person to whom the insurance is payable and they have accepted notice." Had such a letter been written by a lad of twenty without any assistance he must have been unduly precocious.

That mysterious man Scott arrived at Ardlamont on the 8th August. He had sailed from Glasgow in company of Monson, who had given out that the stranger was an engineer come to inspect the boiler of the yacht "Alert," which Monson had chartered for Hambrough. After dinner on the evening of 9th August, Monson and Hambrough went out "splash" fishing in Ardlamont Bay. According to Monson the boat struck a rock and capsized. Hambrough managed to scramble on to it and was rescued by him after he had swum ashore for another boat. Scott watched the fishing operations from the land. In any case there was nothing in this adventure to arouse the suspicion of Hambrough, who treated the matter as a joke, and drank whisky and water with his two companions when they returned to the mansion house in the early morning.

After this exciting experience the trio were out rabbit shooting by seven a.m., although the day was wet and stormy. Both Monson and Hambrough had guns, but Scott had none. Monson usually carried a 12-bore, and Hambrough a short-barrelled 20-bore gun. Before nine o'clock Monson and Scott returned to the mansion house and informed the butler that Hambrough had shot himself and was dead. They had lifted the body and placed it upon the top of a turf dyke. (The death was supposed to have taken place about 7.30 a.m.).

The body was conveyed to the mansion house in a cart by an estate worker, and Dr. Macmillan, of Tighnabruiach, who had previously attended the family, was called. He arrived about 11.30 a.m., and examined the body and the "locus." Monson gave him a detailed description of how the death had occurred. "They had gone out rabbit shooting in a wood, Hambrough taking the right or east side along a turf dyke, Monson the left, and Scott walking in the middle carrying the rabbits. When near the end of the wood he heard a shot fired and called out, 'Have you shot anything?' but he got no reply, and shortly afterwards Scott came up and they turned back together. They had not gone very far along the turf wall until they found Hambrough's body lying in the ditch. There was no sign of life in the body, and the gun was close beside it."

Dr. Macmillan forwarded a report to the Procurator-Fiscal, in which he stated that death was due to an accident; that probably "the deceased walked along the top of the dyke when his foot tripped and the gun went off."

Scott left by the afternoon boat on the same day as the tragedy. Constable M'Calman, who had heard of the fatality, spoke to Scott on the pier at Tighnabruiach and advised him to wait in case there should be an inquiry. Scott, however, said that he had important business and must go, but gave his address as the Central Station Hotel, Glasgow.

Major Hambrough and his wife were wired for and came to Ardlamont. They, along with Monson, accompanied the coffin, which had been ordered from Messrs. Wylie & Lochhead, Glasgow, to Ventnor, Isle of Wight. The silver plate on the lid contained the following inscription:—

"Windsor Dudley Cecil Hambrough,
Lieutenant, 3rd Batt. West Yorks. Regiment,
Aged 20.
Died at Ardlamont from Gun Accident,
10th August, 1893."

It was only after the arrival of two officials of the Mutual Insurance Company of New York at Inveraray, to see the Procurator-Fiscal as to a claim which had been made on the death of Hambrough, that stringent inquiries were instituted by the authorities. Dr. Macmillan, nine days after his first report, made an addition by saying that he accepted the statements of Monson and Scott as correct, believing there was no motive, but now he was of the opinion the injuries could not have been caused in the way he originally thought.

Monson was subsequently arrested by Chief-Constable Fraser, on the 30th August, and emitted the usual declaration before the Sheriff. He was detained in Inveraray Jail until the 8th September, when he was removed to Greenock. The original charge was one of murder, but on the 30th October Monson was taken to Kilmun to emit a second declarattion, which took place in the hotel there before Sheriff Shairp, on the charge of attempting to drown Hambrough. The body of the young lad had been exhumed, and an examination made by Dr. Littlejohn, the well-known medico-legal expert, and Dr. Macmillan.

Now for the trial. It is a remarkable fact, and one which has been alluded to before, that nearly all famous trials before the Justiciary Court at Edinburgh have commenced in inclement weather. Snow, therefore, ushered in the proceedings of the great case. There were no fewer than 110 witnesses for the Crown and 22 for the defence. The principal expert witnesses for the prosecution were Dr. Littlejohn—the papers used to say that no murder trial would be complete without him—Dr. Heron Watson, a veteran of the Crimean War, and Dr. Joseph Bell (the prototype of Sherlock Holmes). Police officers, gamekeepers, fishermen, moneylenders, and George Sweeney, a hall porter at Westminster Palace Hotel, brother of the wanted man, were among the witnesses. The " productions " included guns, cartridges, a rowan, a lime, and a beech sapling. The rowan* was about ten feet in height, and was profusely adorned with red tape, while small pieces of paper were tied to its branches to indicate the pellet marks.

The Crown's theory regarding the murder charge was that Hambrough received the shot in the head from behind, fixed at a distance of nine feet. It was a glancing one from a No. 5 cartridge loaded with amberite powder, discharged from a 12-bore gun. A 12-bore gun, covered with blood, which had been found

---

*The rowan tree is still preserved among the other " productions."

near where the body had lain, at once solved the question as to the bore of the gun. All the medical witnesses for the Crown, including Mr. Macnaughten, gunmaker, Edinburgh, were of opinion that it was quite impossible that the wounds were self-inflicted. Mr. Macnaughten had made a large number of experiments at the "locus" as to the line of fire, with Stewart, the bar officer at Inveraray, as a subject. He also had the gruesome experience of firing at three bodies in the public mortuary to test the various angles from which shots could be fired.

The Procurator-Fiscal gave evidence to the effect that Monson had told him when the tragedy occurred that Hambrough was carrying his usual 20-bore gun, and that they were using amberite cartridges. It was only after making further inquiry that he found there had been an exchange of guns, as no amberite cartridge for a 20-bore gun existed.

Mr. Tottenham spoke as to his advances to Monson to "run the show," as he termed it. It was he who made the claim after Hambrough's death for the insurance on behalf of Mrs. Monson. He said that he knew the Company were not legally liable to pay, as Hambrough was still in his minority. He thought, however, that he might get the money from the Insurance Company by "bluffing," meaning if they did not pay he would spread the report throughout the kingdom that they had quibbled over a strictly technical matter.

Estate servants bore testimony that there were no marks on the undergrowth where Monson alleged he found the body. The keeper who looked after the boat deponed that he was not aware there was a hole in the bottom under the plank until after the tragedy. Police witnesses testified to their efforts to find Scott. These included Inspector Greet of Scotland Yard, who had the assistance of Constable M'Calman for thirteen weeks in London, but they utterly failed to discover him. The brother of the wanted man gave evidence that the family had recently lost sight of him, but "we imagine that he has taken a voyage to Australia for the benefit of his health," said the witness, amidst considerable laughter. Mr. Jerningham had a disagreeable period under cross-examination, when he had to admit that instead of being a man

I

of means all he had came through a marriage settlement, which was not considerable.

Professor Matthew Hay, of Aberdeen University, and Dr. Sanderson, gave evidence for the defence. The latter said, along with Tom Speedy, he made various gun experiments and had visited the "locus." Their evidence was to the effect that the shooting could have been accidental. Mr. Tom Speedy, another expert witness, corroborated. He created some sensation in Court when he stated that he had carried through the experiment of firing a shot through his wife's hair as it lay down her back. This was to negative the Crown's theory that the fatal shot must have been fired at a distance of nine feet, whereas the muzzle must have been within two feet of the victim, as there was no singeing to the hair when he made the experiment.

During the evidence some legal point cropped up, and Mr. Comrie Thomson quoted as an authority from the Lord Justice-Clerk's book on Criminal Law. But the Judge remarked that a person is no authority until he is dead, when, gracefully, the silver-tongued advocate replied, "Well, I hope it will be a long time before you are an authority in that sense."

Mr. Asher, in addressing the jury, marshalled a formidable array of circumstantial evidence. He said Monson was in need of money; he insured the life of Hambrough after many un-successful attempts; his connection with Scott, who had come to Ardlamont to aid in the design; there was also the capsizing of the boat late at night, followed by the shooting tragedy early next morning. Monson, too, had sent the keeper who usually attended him away a message on the morning in question. Again, Monson originally stated that it was a 20-bore gun Hambrough carried, whereas he now said he had exchanged guns, and Hambrough took his 12-bore in order to test a new amberite cartridge. Mr. Asher, in conclusion, said the jury would have to consider whether the facts did not establish the grave and serious chain of events which leads to one result, viz., connecting the prisoner with the crimes.

Mr. Comrie Thomson rose to address the jury on the tenth day of the trial, at 9.30 a.m., the Court having sat one hour earlier than usual (perhaps following a precedent in the Madeleine Smith case). In his opening remarks he said he remembered sitting in those benches five and thirty years ago, hearing John Inglis make his plea for Madeleine Smith. He began his address by words which have become historic, but I repeat them to you now because of their great truth and their wonderful simplicity. "Gentlemen," he said, "the charge against the prisoner is murder, and the punishment for murder is death, and that simple statement is sufficient to suggest to you the awful nature of the occasion which brings you and me face to face." If Mr. Asher stated facts to the jury from which they might well draw only one inference, Mr. Comrie Thomson veritably tore it to tatters. It was the greatest forensic speech since the case to which he had alluded. The learned Advocate said there was really no motive for Monson wishing to kill Hambrough. It was really the very opposite, for in six months, when Hambrough came of age, he would get money from the estates, and there would be plenty for all—the sum might be about £67,000. He held that Monson well knew that under Scots law Hambrough could not assign anything for six months yet, and that Mrs. Monson could not recover any claim that the moneylender had made on the Insurance Company. The family were living on Tottenham's bounty, who expected to be remunerated when Hambrough came of age, while Monson would also share in the money.

"It was one thing essential," said Mr. Comrie Thomson, "that the young man should live. If he died before June, 1894, the whole thing was in the air." He also made a point that the disappearance of Scott was even more unfortunate for the defence than for the Crown. Regarding the boating adventure, Monson had declared that it was Hambrough who cut the hole in the boat to let out the water from the nets. Instead of attempting to drown him, Monson had rescued him. "It was not conceivable," continued the great Advocate, "that Hambrough should be taken out to deep water, the plug removed, even although he succeeded in scrambling ashore, without knowing that an attempt had been made on his life. If an attempt had taken place would he have gone out shooting next morning with the man who made it?"

Regarding the murder, Mr. Comrie Thomson held that the

expert evidence for the Crown was not reliable. "I put it to you," said the learned Advocate, "can any of you say, 'I am certain of the prisoner's guilt, there is no reasonable room for doubting it?'" Mr. Comrie Thomson's final words were: "What would any of you think, if some day—it may be soon—this mystery is entirely unravelled, and it is demonstrated that this man was innocent, while your verdict has sent him to his death? He will not go unpunished if he is guilty. There is One, in whose hands he is, Who is infallible and omniscient: 'I will repay, vengeance is Mine, saith the Lord.'"

The Court rose at 12.30 p.m. for lunch. Thereafter the Lord Justice-Clerk summed up. His Lordship adverted to Monson's mode of life, but said it was a long way from being dishonest to being a murderer. Regarding Scott, he could not see how he had much to do with the case, as the crimes could have been accomplished without him. He might, however, he a hired assassin. His Lordship threw out the suggestion that Scott's visit may have been really a "French invitation," casually given perhaps in a drinking bar. Monson, not wishing to divulge that Scott was a bookmaker's clerk, passed him off as an engineer. It was for the Crown to prove why Scott was there; the onus did not lie with the defence. The whole trend of the Judge's remarks, in both the boating and shooting charges, seemed to be that it would be unsafe to convict. He also drew attention to the evidence of a witness for the defence—a Mr. Donald, who had watched Hambrough on a previous occasion and thought he was careless with the gun.

The jury retired at 3.53 p.m. to consider their verdict. Few who had heard the incisive logic of the Judge thought that when they returned they would be under the baleful shade of the gallows tree, and it was so. After an absence of seventy-three minutes, the jury found both charges not proven. The verdict was received practically without any demonstration. The Lord Justice-Clerk, in thanking the jury, said they would not be called upon again for service. So ended the famous case.

[It has been remarked that Mr. Comrie Thomson did not offer his congratulations to Monson as he stepped from the dock. The strain of conducting the defence in such a gigantic case was no ordinary one, and the great Advocate afterwards remarked, "I do not know whether Monson killed young Hambrough, but I know he nearly killed me."

Scott, who had sentence of fugitation passed upon him, turned up at Edinburgh as a music hall artist some months later. He petitioned the Court to have his sentence revoked, and as there was no appearance for the Crown, the Court granted the order—this was in May, 1894. Monson, too, appeared about this time as an author, when he published a pamphlet, entitled "The Ardlamont Mystery Solved," to which was appended Scott's "diary," which stated that this man of mystery had been present in the High Court every day during the trial. If the diary was true, it was certainly unique to find the "wanted" man sitting quietly in the Court benches while the macer was calling his name three times in the hall and the Judge pronouncing him an outlaw. (Charles Peace, according to a report, went, however, much further, for he sat in Court and heard a man condemned for a crime he himself had committed). The entry in Scott's diary read:—"December 12-20. Have been in Court every day. Ready if wanted, but never had any doubt about the result."

There were over a hundred reporters engaged at the trial—the largest ever known in Scotland. The daily report of the proceedings occupied between fifteen and seventeen columns of "The Scotsman." The Rev. Dr. Whyte, of Free St. George's, Edinburgh, offered up a prayer on behalf of Monson at his Sunday evening service during the trial. For many years, on the anniversary of the tragedy, in the memorial notices of several of the newspapers, appeared the name of Hambrough with the words, "I will repay, vengeance is Mine, saith the Lord."

Lord Kingsburgh, the presiding judge, in his "Jottings," published many years after the trial, makes the following observations on the case. "I went through nine days of anxiety such as I never experienced before or since. The case was one which so bristled with points that one had to watch its course from moment to moment, and to take scrupulous care lest the jury should be misled by feelings roused by the character of the accused. So dominant was the anxiety, that morning after morning I woke long before my usual time and lay in deep perspiration, turning things over and endeavouring to weigh them up and to determine their weight and balance. Never before had I gone through an experience the least like it, and I am well pleased that I had never again a similar experience. It was all the more trying because I felt quite unable to form a determined opinion in my own mind. The way never seemed clear to me. In the end I was able to feel that I had done my best to put the case in a fair light before the jury, and can freely say the verdict they returned was in all the circumstances the safe one. I have been more than comforted by the assurance of judges, including some in other parts of the United Kingdom, that in their opinion the jury were led to the proper conclusion."

Monson figured some years later in the Criminal Courts in England, but this time did not escape, as he was convicted of fraud and sentenced to five years' penal servitude.

A personal note may be added. I well remember the Ardlamont case. I was a boy at school at the time. Coming home each evening I scanned the papers eagerly to see how the case was proceeding. Everyone was talking about it, and I have little doubt that the conversation I heard in those far-off days kindled an interest in matters criminal which has never abated, and has in the end become a life-long study. Among my most treasured possessions are copies of "The Scotsman" with the account of the trial.

I never pass through the Kyles of Bute and round Ardlamont Point but my eyes still scan with undiminished interest the large, white-harled mansion house on the hillside which came so prominently before the public. Through the kindness of the present proprietors I recently had the privilege of visiting Ardlamont. The house is considerably altered, and the surroundings so planted and enclosed that it is now a little difficult to trace the route the sportsmen followed on that tragic morning of the 10th August. The " locus," however, was pointed out to me, but the turf dyke has disappeared. All the employees then on the estate have passed away or left, but relatives of these men are still employed at Ardlamont. In conversation with one, I was informed that one night, when keeping the constable company who was guarding the rowan tree, he heard footsteps outside the tent. On the constable going out the intruder made off. An exciting chase followed, but the man made his escape. Whether this was an attempt to steal the principal " production " was never cleared up. Several other items of interest not generally known I also gathered, but no good purpose would follow by recapitulating them now.

The Ardlamont of to-day ranks as one of the most delightful residences in the west of Scotland, with extensive pleasure grounds and gardens, the herbaceous borders being most luxuriant. Standing on the lawn in front of the house, which glistened in the noonday sunshine on that brilliant day in June, and looking across the Sound of Bute to Arran, created an indelible impression of grandeur and beauty that time will not readily efface. It seems quite incongruous that such an ideal residence should have associations with the darker side of life; even after forty-five years memories of the great case still linger there.]

1894.

June 25. At Dundee Circuit Court, before Lord Kincairney, a somewhat unusual incident occurred. On account of Counsel for the defence not appearing through indisposition, Sheriff-Substitute Campbell-Smith undertook the duties. It is an old custom if there is no Counsel present to represent the defence the Sheriffs must step into the breach. Instances of this procedure are, however, very rare.

1897.

May 17. Before the High Court of Justiciary at Edinburgh, Lord Young on the bench, George Paterson, an old soldier, was convicted of the murder of his paramour in their house at Milton Lane, Glasgow. The details of the tragedy were particularly sordid, as the prisoner had inflicted no fewer than thirty bruises on the woman with a red-hot poker.

The defence, which was in the hands of Mr. Lyon Mackenzie and Mr. Laing (now Sheriff Laing, Aberdeen), attributed the crime to the fact that Paterson had sun-stroke in India, and had lost all self-control. It was by the narrowest of majorities that the capital verdict was returned—eight for murder and seven for culpable homicide. The verdict was also coupled with a unanimous recommendation to mercy on account of provocation. Lord Young passed sentence of death, to be carried out in Duke Street Prison, Glasgow, on the 7th June.

Among the witnesses for the Crown was Sir Henry Littlejohn, the well-known Professor, who on taking his place in the witness-box was greeted with a round of applause from his students, who practically filled the gallery and the body of the Court to the exclusion of the general public. Lord Young sternly commented upon this unseemly conduct, and said it was the duty of the police to take immediately into custody any person guilty of such behaviour.

[It was thought that the Government would not willingly mar the Diamond Jubilee rejoicings with an execution, but the law was allowed to take its course. Lord Balfour of Burleigh was then Home Secretary, and no doubt after consulting with Lord Young found there was not sufficient ground to commute the sentence.

It is remarkable that in none of the four capital cases which came before Lord Young was a reprieve granted. It was also unusual to have a case remitted from Glasgow for trial at Edinburgh except for some special reason, like the Pritchard trial, when local feeling was against him.]

1898.

February 21. Before the High Court of Justiciary at Edinburgh, Lord Young on the bench, John Herdman (52), a printer's machineman, was convicted of the murder of his paramour in a house in Milne's Close, Edinburgh, during a drunken squabble at the New Year. Dr. Littlejohn (afterwards Sir Henry), the police surgeon, described the bruises as the worst he had ever seen. Herdman in addition to kicking the deceased had inflicted several wounds by stabbing.

Mr. Thomson, for the defence, in addressing the jury, said as the most serious part of the evidence against the prisoner was given by little children no absolute reliance could be placed upon it, and therefore asked for a verdict of not proven. After an absence of half-an-hour the jury, by a majority of 10 to 5, found the charge proved.

Lord Young, in passing sentence, said it was no palliation that the prisoner was the worse of drink. Assuming the black cap, his Lordship, in an impressive address, sentenced the prisoner to be hanged within the prison of Edinburgh on the 12th March. Strong efforts to secure a reprieve, and in some districts of the city a house-to-house canvass for signatures, was made. The memorial to Lord Balfour of Burleigh was signed by over 11,000 persons. It, however, proved unavailing. The condemned man, who all along maintained that he remembered nothing about the murder, paid great attention to the ministrations of the Chaplain, the Rev. R. Mackenzie Campbell. The sentence was duly carried out. Billington was the executioner.

1899.

February 14. At Inverness Circuit Court, before Lord Trayner, Allan M'Callum, a noted poacher, was charged with the murder by shooting of Constable King, near Abernethy, and also on the same date, 20th December, attempted to murder Constable Niven by discharging a loaded gun at him. The officers were proceeding to arrest M'Callum for failing to pay a fine for a poaching contravention. On the approach of the constables, M'Callum opened fire with his gun. He then disappeared, but was at length arrested hiding in a straw shed at Tom-na-Croich, Abernethy, after an exhaustive police hunt. Constable King was apprehensive that there would be trouble in arresting M'Callum, and before setting out to make the arrest said to a friend that he hoped M'Callum would not use his gun.

After holding a levee, Lord Trayner was escorted from the Caledonian Hotel to the Castle with much ceremonial. The band of the Cameron Highlanders lead the procession. Charles Kincaid Mackenzie (the late Lord Mackenzie) was Advocate-Depute, while Mr. Blair appeared for the defence. A verdict of culpable homicide on the murder charge and guilty of attempt to murder was returned. Lord Trayner, in passing sentence of fifteen years'

penal servitude, said the jury had taken a very merciful view of
the case.

[This trial excited much public interest in the north, and
even a poem of six stanzas, entitled "Macallum's Lament,"
was composed. The first verse was:—

"Farewell to the hills and dells of Strathspey,
To the dark woods of Tulloch, farewell for aye,
To Nethy's sweet murmur I'll listen no more,
Or scour the dark forests of gloomy Glen More."]

1902.

October 22. At Glasgow Circuit Court, before Lord Trayner
(Old Court), Patrick Leggett (30), was charged with the murder
of his wife at Whiteinch, Glasgow, in September. The crime
was deliberately planned. He had not resided with his wife for
seven years, and had boasted that he would kill her, but "as
there was no hanging nowadays he would probably get fifteen years
for it." (This remark was to some extent true, as there had
been no capital convictions at Glasgow Circuit for ten years, and
within that period quite a number of serious charges of murder
had been before the Courts).

Leggett had gone to the house where his wife resided, and
after inflicting terrible injuries ran out, followed by a crowd who
had been attracted to the scene. In order to avoid capture he
jumped into the Clyde, but was rescued by a ferryman. The
sobering influences of immersion in the water had not diminished
his absolute hatred for her, for when taken to Partick Police Office
he expressed the hope that his wife was dead.

The defence attributed the crime to the fact that the prisoner
was really insane, and that being reared under bad influences
had destroyed his sense of right. After an absence of only five
minutes, the jury returned a unanimous verdict of guilty of
murder. Lord Trayner passed sentence of death, to be carried
out at Duke Street Prison, Glasgow, on the 10th November. His
Lordship, in addressing the Magistrates at the close of the Circuit,
said that some effort should be made to check those crimes so
common in the city.

Although upwards of 10,000 signatures were secured for the petition praying for a reprieve, Lord Balfour of Burleigh refused to intervene. Leggett's grim prophesy was thus not fulfilled. Billington was the executioner.

[Lord Low, who had finished the business in the New Court, had joined Lord Trayner on the bench before sentence was passed.]

1904.

July 5. At Glasgow Circuit Court, before Lord Adam (Old Court), Joseph Calebrere, an ice-cream merchant, was charged with the murder of his wife and family at Kilbirnie in April. In a fit of ungovernable fury, the prisoner committed his terrible deed with a hatchet. His wife had given way to drink and this had preyed upon his mind.

Mr. R. L. Orr (now Sheriff Orr), who conducted the defence, pleaded that the acts were accomplished during an irresistible homicidal impulse. The jury, after an absence of half-an-hour, returned a unanimous verdict of guilty of murder, but with a recommendation to mercy on account of extreme provocation. Lord Adam, in a voice almost inaudible, passed sentence of death, to be carried out within Ayr Prison, on the 26th July. Sentence commuted.

July 5. At Glasgow Circuit Court, before Lord Trayner (New Court), Thomas Gunning was found guilty of the murder of his paramour at Bridgeton, Glasgow. He had reduced the body with blows almost to a mass of bones, and boasted that he had done the act.

Mr. C. N. Johnstone (the late Lord Sands) conducted the defence. The jury, by a majority of 9 to 6, returned a verdict of guilty with a unanimous recommendation to mercy. Sentence of death was pronounced, to take effect within Duke Street Prison, Glasgow, on the 26th July. It was duly carried out by the Brothers Billington, one of whom had come north for the execution of Calebrere at Ayr, before a reprieve was granted.

[Both capital sentences were pronounced within a few minutes of each other, a coincidence without precedent in the annals of the Glasgow Court, the case of Gunning being first. See 1892.]

July 6. At Glasgow Circuit Court, before Lord Adam (Old Court), Adam Black, a Russian Pole, was found guilty of the murder of his son by stabbing him, at Hamilton, in May. The jury, by a majority of 10 to 5, found the prisoner guilty, with a unanimous recommendation to mercy.

Lord Adam passed sentence of death, to be carried out within Duke Street Prison, on the 27th July. Sentence commuted.

[This sitting of the Court in Glasgow has been termed the "Black Assize," as over sixty years had passed since three men had been capitally convicted at one Circuit, and not since 1890 had the last penalty been pronounced in two successive days.]

1905.

October 24. At Glasgow Circuit Court, before Lord Adam (Old Court), Pasha Liffey (20), a Basuto, who went round the country with travelling shows, was charged with the murder of a married woman near Larkhall. Liffey attacked the woman on the road in the dark, criminally assaulted her, and then cut her throat. On the approach of two miners, Liffey made off, when the men discovered the woman lying at the roadside dead. The prisoner, who never left the neighbourhood, was shortly afterwards arrested.

Mr. Orr Deas, Advocate-Depute, characterised the crime as one of the worst which had ever disgraced Lanarkshire. Mr. Laing, for the defence, asked for a verdict of culpable homicide. He said the acts were committed under an uncontrollable impulse when the prisoner was intoxicated. A verdict of guilty was returned by a majority, with a recommendation to mercy. Lord Adam passed sentence of death, to be carried out within Duke Street Prison, Glasgow, on the 14th November.

A petition was forwarded to the Home Secretary praying for a reprieve, which was signed by a number of officers and men of the 2nd Scottish Rifles, as Liffey had been a despatch runner with the regiment in the Boer War. The full penalty was, however, duly inflicted. Pierpoint was the executioner.

1907.

July 3. At Glasgow Circuit Court, before Lord Salvesen (Old Court), James Ritchie (17), was convicted of the murder of a woman in a house in Castle Street, in May. The act was committed while the prisoner was in a state of drunken passion. Ritchie gave himself up to the police shortly afterwards.

His Lordship, in addressing the jury, characterised the tragedy as " one in the lowest strata of Glasgow life, but none the less it was the duty of those who administered the law to see that the humblest and most worthless of her citizens should be free from attack."

Sentence of death was passed but the sentence was commuted.

August 29. At Glasgow Circuit Court, before Lord M'Laren (Old Court), Archibald M'Millan was charged with the murder of a man by stabbing him, in a fish restaurant in the Anderston district of Glasgow.

Lord M'Laren summed up strongly against the prisoner, and indicated this was not a case where a verdict less than murder should be returned. The jury, however, only found the accused guilty of culpable homicide. This was received with a round of applause from the gallery. After the noise had to some extent subsided, his Lordship, with one of his characteristic little coughs, ordered the gallery to be cleared. When a number of persons had been removed, Lord M'Laren said the remainder could stay if they remained quiet. Sentence of penal servitude for life was passed.

[M'Millan, during the summing up of his Lordship, frequently drew his hand across his throat, indicating to his friends that he was going to be hanged. M'Millan died in the Lunatic Department of Perth Penitentiary in July, 1927.]

August 29. At Glasgow Circuit Court, before Lord Guthrie (New Court), Thomas Gray was charged with the murder of his sweetheart in Glasgow. After committing the act he gave himself up to the police. A verdict of culpable homicide was returned. Lord Guthrie, in addressing Gray, said he would have to pronounce the next sentence from that which he had escaped, and that was penal servitude for life.

[This is the only instance of two life sentences being passed
in Glasgow in one day, and pronounced within several minutes
of each other.]

1908.

February 6 and 7. At Aberdeen Circuit Court, before Lord
Mackenzie, Joseph Hume, a deserter from Fort George, was
indicted for the murder of John Barclay Smith, a stone-breaker,
at Lhanbryde, near Elgin, on the 24th September. Mr. A. M.
Anderson, Advocate-Depute (the late Lord Anderson), prosecuted.
Mr. Alexander Moncreiff (now Lord Moncreiff) appeared for the
defence.

Hume, who was penniless, received food, lodgings, and work
from Smith, who lived alone. On Saturday afternoon they both
proceeded to Elgin for provisions. Smith was very much the
worse of drink when they returned, while Hume was sober. When
preparing the evening meal, Smith was so drunk that he had to
lie down in bed. This gave Hume the opportunity for which he
appears to have been waiting. Seizing a mark hammer he struck
his benefactor several blows on the head, reducing it to almost a
pulp. Hume now ransacked the house and took away a gold
watch and all the money that he could lay his hands on. Then
he locked the door and fled.

Several days elapsed before the murder was discovered. Meantime Hume turned up at Edinburgh and visited his sweetheart.
She appeared as one of the Crown witnesses, and bore testimony
to a conversation that she had with him over the watch, which
was no doubt the missing one. When Hume's money was getting
done he attempted to pawn the watch, but the pawnbroker
was suspicious and reported the matter to the police. Hume
disappeared, but was at length captured in a lodging-house in
Stirling, where he had assumed the name of Middleton.

The jury were absent an hour in considering their verdict,
which was unanimous. Lord Mackenzie ordained the prisoner
to be hanged at Inverness on the 5th March. Hume was removed
to the new prison at Porterfield, which had been opened in the
Highland capital in 1902.

Considerable dissatisfaction was occasioned in Inverness
because the sentence was fixed to be carried out there and

not at Aberdeen. Great efforts were made to have the sentence commuted, and a petition containing 7,000 signatures was forwarded to the Home Secretary. The unfortunate man was attended daily by the Rev. Gavin Lang, Chaplain of the prison. In response to a representation made by householders of the residential district which surrounds the prison, the Home Secretary gave orders to dispense with the tolling of the prison bell, but said the black flag would be hoisted. A reprieve was refused, and Hume paid the full penalty. Pierpoint was the executioner.

[This was the first execution in Inverness for over seventy years.]

May 8. At Glasgow Circuit Court, before Lord Ardwall (Old Court), Thomas Bone, junior, was charged with the murder of his wife, on the road leading from Glenbuck village to Muirkirk, on the 2nd April. On being asked to plead, Bone admitted his guilt, and said: "No, I cannot plead not guilty. I have a higher power to face than you, my Lord, and for that I am prepared to plead guilty. It was I who committed the crime."

After a consultation between Lord Ardwall and the Clerk of Court, his Lordship said that he had never heard of such a plea in a murder charge, and evidence required to be led. Witnesses were examined for the prosecution, but there was none for the defence. Counsel for Bone asked for a verdict of culpable homicide. Lord Ardwall, in summing up, said the facts of the case warranted no less a verdict than murder. This was returned by the jury, and sentence of death was passed, to be carried out within Ayr Prison on the 29th May. Sentence commuted.

[This was a very remarkable case. Bone's wife had been in service at various farms near Monkton, and he had frequently been in prison for creating disturbances where she was employed. After wandering about the country, he met his wife by chance at Glenbuck, and induced her to go for a walk with him across the moor. He returned to the village some time afterwards and said that he had killed his wife in a fit of passion. In Court, Bone did not seem to realise the serious position in which he was placed. He laughed and winked to some friends, and even smilingly drew his hands across his throat, purporting that he was going to suffer the last penalty. As it was he escaped the hangman's noose by the matter of some twelve hours.

The scaffold, which had been erected in a joiner's yard, was taken down and removed in sections to the prison on Thursday. The hangman had arrived, and all preparations were complete for the execution on the following day, Friday. But a last minute reprieve was received at Ayr on Thursday night. Bone was subsequently detained in Perth Penitentiary, and latterly became a dangerous lunatic.

Some four years after the trial he hanged himself with a bed sheet which he had attached to a peg in the wall. Bone was the last person under sentence of death who was confined in Ayr Prison, now demolished, so no executions can ever take place again in the "Auld Burgh Toon."]

July 23. At Perth Circuit Court, before Lord Ardwall, Edward Johnstone, a miner, was charged with the murder of a woman named Whithers, with whom he cohabitated at Collyford, Saline, Fife, on the 7th June. The evidence for the prosecution revealed that Johnstone was jealous of the deceased's attention to another man. Three medical witnesses were of opinion that the prisoner was sane at the time libelled. The defence maintained that Johnstone was not fully responsible, due to an over-indulgence in drink.

Lord Ardwall, in summing up, said that jealousy was the strongest motive, and indicated that the prisoner was sane. The jury, after an absence of fifteen minutes, returned a unanimous verdict of guilty, coupled with a strong recommendation to mercy. Sentence of death was passed, to be carried out within Perth Prison on the 19th August.

After the trial, Johnstone expressed the hope that there would be no reprieve, but afterwards wished that the petition sent to Lord Pentland would be successful. The petition, which was signed by fourteen members of the jury, contained in all 639 signatures, while in addition there was also another petition from Castledown, Londonderry, his native place, which contained 1,590 names.

The Glasgow scaffold was borrowed by the authorities, and was erected in the store room at the north wall of the prison.

The Rev. Walter E. Lee, Chaplain, visited the condemned man, and was most assiduous in his ministerial attentions. A reprieve was refused. The execution was carried through by Ellis and his assistant, Willis.

[This was the first execution in Perth since 1870. I was present at the trial. Lord Ardwall summed up against the prisoner, and the capital verdict was thus not unexpected. It seemed almost hours, although it could only be the matter of several minutes, before the Clerk of Court had written out the death sentence on the Court Record. A pin could almost be heard to drop; there is no sound in the hushed Court except the scratching pen of the Clerk hurrying over the old-world formula in the leather-bound book of doom. The Clerk has finished writing, and the macer hands the book to his Lordship, who, assuming the black cap, in clear and distinct tones reads out the sentence. The tension is over, the prisoner is removed below, and the crowd slowly disperses. Those who have witnessed such a scene will probably remember it to their dying day. It is horribly fascinating, hideously impressive and dramatic.

The painful interval after a capital sentence is returned, and before sentence is passed is now obviated by having the death sentence prepared on a sheet of paper, and is thus read out by the Judge immediately the verdict is passed. After the prisoner is removed, the verdict is duly inscribed in the Court Record and signed by the Judge.

The Circuit was noteworthy as the first occasion the erstwhile Sheriff of Perthshire, Mr. Andrew Jamieson, had visited the city as a Circuit Judge since being promoted to the Bench. In his honour a new flag floated from the flagstaff on the County Buildings. The Circuit continued for two days, when several cases involving heavy sentences of penal servitude were disposed of.]

August 24 and 25. At Inveraray Circuit Court, before Lord Johnston, a charge of murder and attempt to murder was set down for trial. Mr. T. B. Morison, Advocate-Depute, appeared for the Crown, while Mr. Constable conducted the defence in both cases. Both these gentlemen were promoted to the Bench, but Lord Constable died in 1928, while Lord Morison has retired.

In the attempt to murder charge, which was from Dunoon,

K

it was intimated the prisoner was insane and unable to instruct a defence. The accused was ordered to be detained during His Majesty's pleasure.

The other charge related to a local doctor meeting a violent death on the road near Ardrishaig. After the luncheon interval on the 25th, Mr. Constable intimated that the prisoner would plead guilty to culpable homicide. This was accepted by the Crown, and Lord Johnston passed sentence of seven years' penal servitude.

[As this was the first sitting of the High Court at Inveraray since the 25th March, 1887 (which was a maiden Court), great interest was manifested in the trials. All the old-world pageantry associated with the Circuit Court in bygone times was revived. Lord Johnston arrived at the burgh boundary on Friday, the 21st, and according to ancient custom was met by the Provost and Magistrates of the Royal Burgh, accompanied by two halberdiers, who escorted the Judge to his "lodgings," the Argyll Arms Hotel.

Lord Johnston held a levee in the hotel before proceeding to the Court on the Monday. A procession was formed outside. The local company of the 8th Battalion Argyll and Sutherland Highlanders acted as a guard of honour. The procession was led by the two town officers of Inveraray, in antique scarlet-coat uniforms, bearing the burgh halberds. Lord Johnston was accompanied in the procession and to the Bench by the Duke of Argyll, as Lord Lieutenant of the County. Sheriff M'Lure and other County officials took part in the procession, which proceeded by the main street to the Courthouse. The prisoner was guarded in the dock by constables and halberdiers on each side.

It may be added that Lord Johnston had an interesting connection with Inveraray, as his grand-uncle on his mother's side was long resident Sheriff-Substitute and also Provost. Although the institution of the High Court of Justiciary dates back to 1588, Inveraray was then not included as a Circuit town. The Dukes of Argyll, as hereditary judges of their own district, held regular Courts themselves until the reign of George II. The first sitting of the Circuit Court was inaugurated by an unique ceremony, as the Judge and several of the Court officials, including the macer, were admitted burgesses of the burgh. In the early "sixties" an agitation commenced to have the County business removed to Dunoon on account of convenience, and also because the popular Clydeside resort was rapidly increasing, whereas Inveraray was looked upon as a decaying town. The proposed change was strenuously opposed by George, sixth Duke of Argyll, and it was not until two years after his death, in 1900, that the County business was removed to Dunoon. Inveraray is still a Circuit Court, although few sittings take place. The custom of fixing the Spring and Autumn Circuits in the old County town is, however, still observed.

The last sitting of the High Court at Inveraray was held on the 27th March, 1934, after an interval of twenty-five years. Once again all the old Justiciary customs were revived—the levee, the procession, and the two halberdiers on each side of the constables guarding the prisoner in the dock.]

1909.

July 8 and 9. At Perth Circuit Court, before Lord Guthrie, Alexander Edminstone (23), an unemployed miner, was charged with having, on the 19th February, robbed a young lad, named Michael Swinton Brown, of £85 in money, also a watch and chain, and further, at the same time and place, "within the lavatory at East Wemyss, Fife, did murder him." Mr. A. M. Anderson, K.C., Advocate-Depute (the late Lord Anderson), prosecuted, while the defence was conducted by Mr. J. A. Christie and Mr. Armit.

Brown, who was a clerk at East Wemyss, had been in the habit of going to the bank every Friday for money for his employer's wages. This had become known to Edminstone, and he dogged the lad's footsteps from the bank to the tramway car and travelled with him. Edminstone and the lad went into the lavatory together, and probably when the money was not handed over at his request he strangled him. Suspicion fell upon Edminstone, who had disappeared. Traces were discovered of his movements at Strathmiglo, Perth and Glasgow. The leather bag which had contained the money and the bank pass-book was found on the sea shore near Macduff's Castle.

After extensive police inquiries extending over several weeks, the wanted man was located living in lodgings in Manchester, where he had assumed the name of "Albert Edwards." In a gladstone bag was found a considerable amount of the missing money—£25 in single bank notes, £10 10/- in gold, and £7 5/- in silver. The man admitted that he was Edminstone, but said that when he committed the acts he did not know what he was about.

A defence of insanity was put forward at the trial. Evidence was brought to show that the prisoner had previously suffered from epileptic fits. In addressing the jury, Mr. Christie made a strong appeal to find the accused only guilty of culpable homicide on account of his delusions and diminished responsibility. After an absence of only ten minutes, the jury returned with a unanimous verdict of guilty of murder. Lord Guthrie thereupon passed sentence of death, to be carried out within Perth Prison on the 6th July.

A petition was forwarded to the Home Secretary asking that the sentence should be commuted, but taking in all the circumstances, and also the fact that there was no recommendation from the jury to mercy, this was refused. Edminstone went to his doom. Ellis was the executioner.

1910.

April 12 and 13. At Perth Circuit Court, before Lord Low, Robert Ford Duff, a bottle blower, was charged with the murder of his step-daughter, 4½ years, by beating, kicking, and throwing her over a fence at Craigie, Perth. Probably the crime would not have been brought to light had it not been for the astuteness of Dr. Fraser Bisset. When the prisoner and his wife came to him to get a medical certificate for the child's death, he was not satisfied with the explanation. The doctor said he would call next day and see the body. After doing so he came to the conclusion that the bruises could not be accounted for by an epileptic fit, as he had been informed. He was of the opinion that death had ensued from external violence, and refused to grant a certificate. The police were informed, and in the course of inquiries discovered a person who saw the accused kick an object three times, which turned out to be the child.

The prisoner, who was dressed in a suit of mourning, which he had no doubt donned in memory of his late charge, pleaded not guilty. Mr. W. Lyon Mackenzie was Advocate-Depute, while Mr. D. M'Kechnie and Mr. R. Candlish Henderson appeared for the defence. Mr. R. Macgregor Mitchell (the late Lord Macgregor Mitchell, of the Scottish Land Court) was the local agent for the accused. Evidence was led. There seemed to be no apparent motive for the murder. It was said that Duff, being of a low, degraded nature, probably had given excessive punishment.

Lord Low, in charging the jury, said that death following persistent abuse by kicking and_thrashing amounted to murder, even although the prisoner did not really intend to murder the child. After an absence of fifteen minutes, the jury found the charge proved, accompanied by a recommendation to mercy. Lord Low passed sentence of death, to be carried out within Perth Prison on the 10th May. The prisoner collapsed on hearing the sentence, and had to be carried from the dock in a fainting condition. The death penalty was commuted.

October 18. At Glasgow Circuit Court, before Lord Ardwall (Old Court), Sulleyman Adam (23), a lascar (a native of Bombay territory), was charged with the murder of the "serang," or boatswain (the man on the steamer who looked after the coolies), on board the "Newby Hall," of Liverpool, while berthed in Queen's Dock, Glasgow, on the 27th August.

The prisoner, who wore a white linen jacket and trousers and was barefooted, pleaded not guilty. Superintendent Martin, of the Lanarkshire Constabulary (afterwards Chief Constable of Perthshire) was appointed interpreter. From the evidence it appeared a quarrel had taken place among the coolies, and when the deceased interfered the prisoner stabbed him. Lord Ardwall, in summing up, said the evidence did not justify a verdict of culpable homicide. The jury, by a majority, found the accused guilty, with a strong recommendation to mercy. His Lordship, having assumed the black cap, formally read the death sentence, and handed the sheet of paper to the interpreter. The sentence was, however, commuted.

[This Circuit was held in the County Buildings, as the Justiciary Buildings, opened in 1812, were meantime undergoing renovations. The case was tried in the J.P. Court Hall.]

INDEX.

APPENDIX I.

List of Executions, with Year.

(a Denotes the case is mentioned previously in this book under Trials.)

Aberdeen—

John Young. Murder	1801
Andrew Hossach. Robbery	1810
a John Ritchie (17). Sheep Stealing	1818
a John Barnett. Theft	1818
Robert Mackintosh. Murder	1821
William Gordon. Murder	1821
a George Thom. Murder	1821
William Gordon. Wife Murder	1822
Robert Gordon. Murder	1822
Triple execution—Donaldson, Buchanan and M'Leod. Theft and Stouthrief	1823
Alexander Martin. Theft and Stouthrief	1824
William Allen. Murder and Robbery	1826
a Malcolm Gillespie. Forgery, etc.	1827
a Mrs. Humphrys. Murder	1830
a James Burnett. Wife Murder	1849
a James Robb. Murder	1849
a George Christie. Murder	1852
a John Booth. Murder	1857

Ayr—

Matthew Lay. Murder	1800
William Dornan. Housebreaking	1809
Robert Smith. Housebreaking	1809
John M'Millian. Murder	1810
a George Watson. Horse Stealing	1811
M'Manus and Gibson. Highway Robbery	1814
John Worthington. Robbery (at Symington Toll)	1815
a William Robertson. Robbery and Theft	1817
a Joseph Cairns. Robbery and Theft	1817
a Margaret Crossan. Fire Raising	1817
James Burtnay. Rape	1822
Anderson and Glen. Murder	1823
James Austin. Uttering Forged Notes	1827
a Samuel Waugh. Murder	1832
a James M'Whellan. Murder	1848
a Alexander Cunningham. Murder	1854

Cupar—

William Robertson. Rape	1824
a John Henderson. Murder	1830
a Michael and Peter Scanlan. Murder	1852
a William M'Donald. Murder	1878

DALKEITH—

   a William Thomson. Highway Robbery   -   -   1827

DUMBARTON—

   a Patrick Lunnay. Murder   -   -   -   -   1860
   a David Wardlaw. Wife Murder   -   -   -   1875

DUMFRIES—

   Maitland Smith. Murder   -   -   -   -   1807
   a Edward M'Rory. Assault and Robbery   -   -   1820
   a James Gordon. Murder   -   -   -   -   1821
   John M'Canna and Joseph Robertson. Forgery   -   1823
   James M'Manus. Assault and Robbery   -   -   1826
   a Mary Timney. Murder   -   -   -   -   1862
   a Robert Smith. Murder -   -   -   -   -   1868

DUNDEE—

   John West. Housebreaking   -   -   -   -   1801
   David Balfour. Wife Murder -   -   -   -   1826
   a Arthur Wood. Murder -   -   -   -   -   1839
   a Thomas Leith. Wife Murder -   -   -   -   1844
   a William Henry Bury. Wife Murder -   -   -   1889

EDINBURGH— ,

   a Thomas Urquhart. Opening Letters -   -   -   1800
   Richard Brodie. Theft -   -   -   -   -   1801
   a Andrew Lawrie. Theft of Money from Letters   -   1802
   George Lindsay. Murder   -   -   -   -   1802
   a Margaret Masson. Murder   -   -   -   -   1806
   a Smith and Stevenson. Horse Stealing -   -   -   1807
   Margaret Cunningham. Murder   -   -   -   1807
   Barbara Malcolm. Murder   -   -   -   -   1808
   Robert Stewart. Housebreaking and Theft -   -   1809
   John Armstrong. Housebreaking and Theft -   -   1810
   Adam Lyall. Highway Robbery   -   -   -   1811
   a Triple execution—M'Donald, Sutherland and M'Intosh.
      Murder and Robbery   -   -   -   -   1812
   a M'Donald and Black. Highway Robbery (at Colt-
      bridge)   -   -   -   -   -   -   1813
   a Christina Sinclair. Child Murder   -   -   -   1813
   James M'Dougall. Forgery   -   -   -   -   1814
   a Kelly and O'Neil. Highway Robbery (at Braidburn)   1815
   John Murdoch. Murder -   -   -   -   -   1815
   David Thomson. Housebreaking and Theft -   -   1816
   a Robert Johnstone. Robbery   -   -   -   -   1818
   George Warden. Theft of Money from Letters   -   1819
   a Bryce Judd and Thomas Clapperton. Hamesucken   1819
   a James Whiteford. Hamesucken   -   -   -   1819
   John Dempsey. Wife Murder -   -   -   -   1820
   Samuel Maxwell. Robbery   -   -   -   -   1820
   a David Haggart. Murder   -   -   -   -   1821
   Rennie and Sutherland. Housebreaking and Theft -   1821
   a Mary M'Kinnon. Murder   -   -   -   -   1823
   Andrew Fullerton. Assault and Robbery   -   -   1826
   a William Burke. Murder   -   -   -   -   1828
   a John Stewart and his Wife. Murder -   -   -   1829

L

EDINBURGH—continued.

William Adam. Robbery - - - -	1830
a Robert Edmund. Murder - - - -	1830
John Thomson and David Dobbie. Murder, etc. -	1830
James Low and Thomas Beveridge. Murder, etc. -	1831
John M'Court. Wife Murder - - - -	1831
a George Gilchrist. Coach Robbery - - -	1831
John Howison. Murder - - - -	1831
James Bell. Murder - - - -	1835
Elizabeth Banks. Husband Murder - - -	1835
Charles Donaldson. Wife Murder - - -	1836
a James Wemyss. Wife Murder - - -	1840
a James Bryce. Murder - - - -	1844
a William Bennison. Wife Murder - - -	1850
a William Cumming. Wife Murder - - -	1854
a George Bryce. Murder - - - -	1864
a Eugene Marie Chantrelle. Wife Murder - -	1878
a Robert Flockart Vickars and William Innes. Murder	1884
a Jessie King. Murder - - - -	1889
a John Herdman. Murder - - - -	1898

ELGIN—

a William Noble. Murder - - - -	1834

FALKIRK—

a Thomas M'Nair. Robbery - - - -	1811

FAN'S FARM, BERWICKSHIRE—

a Robert Scott. Murder - - - -	1823

FORFAR—

a Margaret Wishart. Murder - - -	1827
a James Robertson. Murder - - - -	1848

GLASGOW—

a Peter Greig. Hamesucken - - - -	1800
William Cunningham. Theft - - - -	1803
David Scott and Hugh Adamson. Forgery - -	1805
Adam Cox. Murder - - - -	1807
James Gilchrist. Murder - - - -	1808
John Gordon M'Intosh and George Stewart. House-breaking - - - - -	1809
James Ferguson. Robbery - - - -	1813
William Muir and William Moodie. Robbery -	1813
William Higgins and Thomas Harrold. Robbery -	1814
John Sherry. Murder - - - -	1815
John Black. Assault and Robbery - - -	1817
William Baird and Walter Blair. Assault and Robbery	1818
a Matthew Clydesdale. Murder - - - -	1818
a Quintuple execution—M'Kinlay, Guthrie, Forbes, Buchanan and Roberts. Housebreaking -	1819
a John Buchanan. Murder - - - -	1819
a James Wilson. Treason - - - -	1820
a Quadruple execution—Grant, Crosbie, Connor and M'Colgan. Housebreaking - - -	1820
Triple execution—M'Intyre, Paterson and Dyer. Housebreaking - - - -	1821
William Campbell. Housebreaking - - -	1822

GLASGOW—continued.

Thomas Donnachy. Housebreaking and Theft	-	1822
James Campbell. Housebreaking - - -		1822
M'Donald and Wilson. Housebreaking and Theft	-	1823
David Whyte. Housebreaking and Theft -	-	1823
William M'Creevie. Uttering Forged Notes -	-	1824
William Devan. Murder - - -	-	1824
James Stevenson. Assault and Robbery	-	1825
John Dollan. Robbery - - -	-	1826
Kelby and Stewart. Assault and Robbery	-	1826
Edward Moore. Murder - - -	-	1828
William Porter and John Hill. Assault and Robbery		1830
David Little. Stouthrief - - -	-	1831
James Campbell. Housebreaking -	-	1831
James Bryce and his Wife. Murder - -	-	1831
a William Heath. Robbery - - -	-	1831
William Lindsay. Murder - -	-	1832
George Doffey. Wife Murder - -	-	1832
Henry Burnett. Murder - -	-	1833
Hugh Kennedy. Attempt to Murder -	-	1834
George Campbell. Murder - -	-	1835
Mrs. Jaffray. Murder - - -	-	1837
Thomas Templetoun. Wife Murder - -	-	1840
a Doolan and Reeding. Murder (at Bishopbriggs)	-	1841
Charles Mackay. Wife Murder - -	-	1843
a Mrs. Hamilton. Murder - -	-	1850
a Archibald Hare. Murder - - -	-	1851
a Hans Smith M'Farlane and Helen Blackwood.		
Murder - - - - -	-	1853
a John Reilly. Murder - - -	-	1863
a Dr. Pritchard. Murder - - -	-	1865
a Patrick Docherty. Murder - -	-	1875
a Thomas Bass. Murder - - -	-	1876
a Henry Mullen and Martin Scott. Murder	-	1883
a Henry Delvin. Murder - - -	-	1890
a William M'Keown. Murder - -	-	1892
a George Paterson. Murder - -	-	1897
a Patrick Leggett. Murder - -	-	1902
a Thomas Gunning. Murder - -	-	1904
a Pasha Liffey. Murder - - -	-	1905

GREENLAW—

a Mannes Swiney. Assault and Robbery -	-	1834
a John Williams. Murder - -	-	1853

GREENOCK—

Moses M'Donald. Housebreaking - -	-	1812
a Triple execution—Three Irishmen. Housebreaking, etc.		1817
John Kerr. Murder - - -	-	1827
a John Boyd. Wife Murder - -	-	1834
a Frederick Thomas Storey. Murder - -	-	1891

HAWICK—

John Gibson. Murder - - -	-	1814

INVERARAY—

a Peter M'Dougal. Murder - -	-	1807

INVERNESS—

   a Alexander Gillan. Murder, etc.   -   -   -   1810
     Andrew Cullen. Child Murder -   -   -   1813
   a Hector M'Leod. Murder   -   -   -   1831
   a John Adam. Murder   -   -   -   -   1835
   a Joseph Hume. Murder -   -   -   -   1908

JEDBURGH—

     Charles Mercer. Murder   -   -   -   1809
     Thomas Roger. Murder   -   -   -   1831
   a Thomas Wilson. Murder   -   -   -   1849

KINGHORN—

   a John Westwater. Murder   -   -   -   1806

SANDS OF LEITH—

   a Heaman and Gautier. Murder and Piracy   -   1821

LINLITHGOW—

   a Ralph Woodness. Housebreaking   -   -   1819
   a Peter M'Lean. Murder -   -   -   -   1857

MONTROSE—

   a Margaret Shuttleworth. Murder   -   -   1821
   a Andrew Brown. Murder   -   -   -   1866

PAISLEY—

     Craig and Brown. Stouthrief -   -   -   1829
   a William Pirrie. Murder   -   -   -   1837
   a John Thomson. Murder   -   -   -   1857

PERTH—

   a Donald M'Craw. Murder   -   -   -   1806
   a Triple execution—Larg, Mitchell, and Steel. House-
        breaking   -   -   -   -   1817
     Wyllie and Clark. Housebreaking   -   -   1817
   a John Chisholm. Wife Murder -   -   -   1832
   a John Kellocher. Murder   -   -   -   1849
   a Joseph Bell. Murder   -   -   -   -   1866
   a George Chalmers. Murder   -   -   -   1870
   a Edward Johnstone. Murder   -   -   -   1908
   a Alexander Edminstone. Murder   -   -   -   1909

STIRLING—

     Alexander O'Cain. Robbery   -   -   -   1812
     James Campbell. Robbery   -   -   -   1819
   a Andrew Hardie and John Baird. Treason   -   1820
   a John Fleming. Forgery   -   -   -   1821
     John M'Graddy. Housebreaking   -   -   1826
   a Alexander Miller. Murder   -   -   -   1837
   a Allen Mair. Murder   -   -   -   -   1843

APPENDIX II.

EXTRACT FROM THE RECORD OF BURIALS IN THE EDINBURGH AND LEITH CEMETERY AT ROSEBANK.

Date of Interment.	No.	Surname.	Name and Designation.	Place of Nativity.	Funeral proceeded from	Interred in Compartment.	Interred in No.	Interred in Private or Common Ground.	Interred in Depth.	Date of Decease.	Age. Years.	Age. Months.	Disease.
17th April, 1850.	1128	Hamilton,	Jane, Spouse of Wm. Bennison (smith).	Leith?	Steads Place.	P.	173	Com.		April 15th, 1850.	40		Consumption.

That the above is a true extract from the Record of Burials in the said Edinburgh and Leith Cemetery at Rosebank, is certified by me the Recorder of Burials and Superintendent of the Cemetery Grounds.

Witness my hand at Edinburgh the 30th day of January, One Thousand Nine Hundred and Thirty-seven years.

(Sgd.)   S. A. ROWDEN,

Superintendent.